W9-BTQ-657

Fresh from the

Vegetarian
Slow Cooker

Other books by Robin Robertson

Vegan Planet

The Vegetarian Meat & Potatoes Cookbook

Pasta for All Seasons

Rice & Spice

The Sacred Kitchen (with Jon Robertson)

The Vegetarian Chili Cookbook

Some Like It Hot

The Soy Gourmet

366 Simply Delicious Dairy-Free Recipes

365 Healthful Ways to Cook Tofu and Other Meat Alternatives

Fresh from the
Vegetarian
Slow Cooker

200 Recipes for

Healthy and Hearty

One-Pot Meals

That Are Ready When You Are

Robin Robertson

The Harvard Common Press
Boston, Massachusetts

The Harvard Common Press
535 Albany Street
Boston, Massachusetts 02118
www.harvardcommonpress.com

Copyright © 2004 by Robin Robertson
Illustrations copyright © 2004 by Neverne Covington
Crock-Pot® is a registered trademark of The Holmes Group.

All rights reserved. No part of this publication may be reproduced or transmitted in any form
or by any means, electronic or mechanical, including photocopying, recording, or any information
storage or retrieval system, without permission in writing from the publisher.

Printed in the United States

Library of Congress Cataloging-in-Publication Data

Robertson, Robin (Robin G.)
   Fresh from the vegetarian slow cooker : 200 recipes for healthy and hearty one-pot meals
that are ready when you are / Robin Robertson.
      p.   cm.
   Includes index.
   ISBN 1-55832-255-8 (hc : alk. paper)—ISBN 1-55832-256-6 (pbk : alk. paper)
   1. Vegetarian cookery   2. Electric cookery, Slow.   I. Title.
   TX837.R62493   2004
   641.5'636—dc22   2003017320

   ISBN-13: 978-1-55832-256-1
   ISBN-10: 1-55832-256-6

Special bulk-order discounts are available on this and other Harvard Common Press books.
Companies and organizations may purchase books for premiums or resale, or may arrange a
custom edition, by contacting the Marketing Director at the address above.

15 14 13 12 11

Cover recipe: Spicy White Bean and Sweet Potato Stew with Collards, page 70
Back cover recipes: Winter Squash Stuffed with Couscous, Apricots, and Pistachios, page 155,
and Chocolate Fantasy Fondue, page 231

Cover design by Night & Day Design
Cover photographs by Susie Cushner Photography
Interior design by Ralph L. Fowler
Illustrations by Neverne Covington

Contents

Acknowledgments

I am grateful to my diligent and dedicated recipe testers, who often piloted as many as three slow cookers at one time: Gloria Siegel, Linda Levy Elsenbaumer, and Janet Aaronson; as well as their helpers and tasters: Mel Siegel, Ron Elsenbaumer, Gerald Aaronson, Anita Vanetti, Jamie Mowry, John Mowry, Fran Levy, and Monte Shaw. Much gratitude also goes to my husband, Jon Robertson, my own in-house helper and taster, for his willingness to chop mountains of vegetables and taste numerous recipes—often more than once. Special thanks to my sister Carole Lazur, my niece Kristen Lazur, my friends Pat Davis, Kay and Larry Sturgis, and especially Samantha Ragan for inspiring me to become reacquainted with the slow cooker. I also want to thank the entire staff at The Harvard Common Press and my agent, Stacey Glick, of Dystel and Goderich Literary Management. A grateful acknowledgment also goes to the West Bend Company for providing one of the slow cookers used to develop and test the recipes.

Introduction

The true appeal of using a slow cooker is in its simplicity and convenience. Just plug it in, turn it on, and this self-contained, small appliance cooks your entire dinner while you do other things. As they say—set it and forget it. When you return several hours later, your kitchen is filled with the welcoming fragrance of a home-cooked meal. It feels as if you have a personal chef who cooked all day while you were at work or out shopping.

No longer just a way to cook tough cuts of meat, slow cookers are now used to prepare everything from breakfast to bread pudding. They are also ideal for vegetarian cooking, because slow cooking is a convenient way to prepare many bean and grain dishes, as well as other meatless recipes. In addition to convenience, slow cooking scores high marks for taste and nutrition, since the long cooking time allows the nutrients to concentrate in the food, while drawing more flavor out of the ingredients.

The interesting paradox of a slow cooker is that while the food takes longer to cook, the cook has more free time. It is such a liberating feeling to put dinner on to cook in the morning, knowing it will be ready when you are—no more rushing home to get dinner started. Best of all, using a slow cooker can actually help you to eat more well-balanced and economical meals on the nights when you're running late or too tired to cook—the times when we tend to opt for take-out, junk food, or some other convenience food. With just a little planning, I like to think that slow cooking provides the ultimate convenience food.

As you explore the pages of *Fresh from the Vegetarian Slow Cooker*, you'll discover that slow cooking goes way beyond the expected soups and stews. With chapters on everything from appetizers to main dishes, beverages to desserts, there's something for everyone for breakfast, lunch, and dinner. As I developed and tested these recipes, I became increasingly impressed with the virtues of vegetarian slow cooking. I have no doubt that when you lift the lid of your slow cooker for the first time, the intoxicating aromas and flavors will make you a believer, too.

Slow Cooker Basics, Vegetarian Style

. . .

Whoever said, "Everything old is new again" may well have had slow cookers in mind. During the early 1970s, a slow cooker, or Crock-Pot, graced many kitchen counters, taking on the job of cooking dinner while we were at work. It was a convenient and easy way to prepare recipes that usually required more time than was available. Eventually, however, many of us banished our slow cookers to the attic. I'm not sure why—maybe they just didn't seem "cool" anymore.

I admit that I didn't give my Crock-Pot much thought until a few years ago, when I noticed a resurgent interest in the new and improved slow cookers. My old cooker had long since been sold at a yard sale, and I wasn't sure I needed yet another small appliance in my already crowded kitchen. Besides, I had come to associate slow cookers with tough cuts of meat and, as a vegetarian, I had dismissed it as something I could live without.

Then one day an especially busy friend of mine told me about all the fabulous vegetarian dishes she was making in her new slow cooker. Sam went on about the intoxicating fragrances that welcomed her each night as she came home from work. Savory soups, stews, and bean dishes that she otherwise would not have the time to make—not even with a pressure cooker—were being concocted in her slow cooker. I began to see the slow cooker in a new light and was intrigued by the possibilities. The next day, I bought myself a sleek black and stainless steel slow cooker. It sure looked better than my harvest gold model of the past. But I soon discovered that this new style of cooker was more than just a pretty face. The thing could cook and, it seemed, think a little, too. (It automatically turns itself to "warm" after it is done cooking for the preset amount of time.)

From the first pot of soup I made in the new cooker, I was hooked, and for more reasons than the mere convenience. I was compelled by something more basic and primal—it hearkens back to the old iron pot on the hearth of our ancestors. Without fail, whenever I start a slow-cooked meal, a warm "back to my roots" feeling comes over me. This should come as no surprise when you think about how long-cooked, slow-simmered foods have been the hallmark of many global cuisines, including many humble soups and stews such as the cassoulet, tian, and tagine.

While the slow cooker was once synonymous with cooking pot roasts and other meat dishes, the vegetarian cook will find a vast number of ways to use it, just as my friend discovered. Beyond the usual vegetarian soups, stews, chilis, and bean dishes, you can make braised vegetables, risottos, porridges, casseroles, chutneys, relishes, breads, and even desserts. Some of the recipes in this book draw from classic recipes, retooled for the vegetarian, while others are my own favorite vegetarian recipes adapted to the slow cooker, resulting in great flavor and incredible convenience. That's what I like best about slow cooker vegetarian recipes: The long, slow-cooking process enriches the flavor of the dish in a way that other cooking methods can't match. The deep complex flavors of stews and chilis, prepared on the stovetop, for example, pale in comparison to the slow-cooked version.

Why Use a Slow Cooker?

Singles, couples, and families all enjoy slow cooker cooking, and the reasons are as varied as the people who use them. Most slow cooker enthusiasts agree, however, that convenience, economy, and great taste are what keep them coming back to their slow cooker time and again. Simply assemble your ingredients in the slow cooker, turn it on, and that's it. In addition, the ceramic insert can be refrigerated, so you can prepare your ingredients the night before and refrigerate them overnight right in the insert. For further convenience, you can also serve your meal from the ceramic insert. As more people juggle trying to eat healthier with their busy lifestyles, they may find that vegetarian slow cooking provides an answer.

Slow cookers are especially useful for preparing vegetarian meals because of how well they cook many bean, grain, and vegetable dishes. While some people may prefer using a pressure cooker for beans and other long-cooking recipes, it's hard to beat the convenience of a slow cooker that you can leave unattended—something you wouldn't do with a pressure cooker or any other stove-top cooking method. Although meals prepared in a slow cooker take longer to cook, they can actually save you time.

Then there is the flavor factor. A dish that has been simmered for hours in a slow cooker can actually taste better than the same recipe prepared quickly on top of the stove. The reason is the extended, gentle cooking time in the lidded ceramic insert. Cooking this way allows the flavors of the ingredients to fully come out, mingle, and intensify. Using a slow cooker allows you to enjoy the intense "slow-cooked" flavors of hearty soups, stews, and other recipes without out the bother of "slaving over a hot stove." In addition, a slow cooker doesn't heat up the kitchen the way the stovetop or oven does, a definite plus when you're cooking on hot days. Finally, the slow cooker uses less energy, so you save money on utilities.

Slow cooking can also save you money on ingredients because it makes it easy to cook economical bean dishes and make larger quantities of food that can be frozen for a quick easy meal instead of relying on more expensive convenience foods. And, you may actually enjoy cooking more. For example, while your main dish is simmering in the slow cooker, you've got more time available to be creative with your side dishes, salads, or other accompaniments.

Since slow cooking is an ideal way to prepare soups, stews, and bean dishes, you'll be more inclined to eat these healthier choices rather than grabbing something less nourishing because it's quick. When you put food on to slow cook, it can be ready to eat when you are. Food won't burn when left unattended because the heating coils in slow cookers cook food gently and evenly from the bottom and sides. The lid helps keep the heat inside to get the job done without someone to tend to it. While the benefits of this are obvious when you're not home, it's also a great relief to busy stay-at-home moms and others who may be home, but don't have the time to linger in the kitchen.

Versatility is another great reason to slow cook. Thanks to the wide variety of sizes now available, slow cookers can be used to make anything from appetizers to desserts. A slow cooker can also be a great help when company's coming, allowing you to keep the soup or main dish warm while you entertain your guests. Using a slow cooker also lets you free up other cooking surfaces. This can be especially handy for holiday meals. If you're having a buffet, you can put the slow cooker right on the table. It will keep the food at the proper serving temperature for hours while you enjoy the party. Slow-cooked dishes are also great to take along to potlucks—just bring the entire thing along and plug it in when you get there to serve your dish warm.

All About Slow Cookers

Slow cookers come in sizes ranging from one to seven quarts and are available in round or oval shapes. The most popular sizes are the 3½- to 4-quart and the 5½- to 6-quart. The best size cooker to use is indicated in each of my recipes, with most calling for the 3½- to 4-quart size, which comfortably makes enough food for four to six servings. The larger models are great for large quantities of food and also to hold racks and pans for baking in the slow cooker. The smaller, 1- to 1½-quart size is ideal for dips and other party food but is impractical for most everyday cooking. Many recipes in this book will call for a 4-quart slow cooker. In most cases, the recipe will also work fine in a 3½-quart model, as well as a 5½- to 6-quart model, with little or no adjustment. (Do keep in mind that slow cookers work best when at least half full—and the ingredients in most recipes for a 4-quart cooker will be enough to half fill a 6-quart cooker.)

The removable ceramic insert of the slow cooker is dishwasher, oven, and microwave safe, but cannot be used directly on the stovetop. The slow cooker unit has High and Low settings instead of temperature dials. You can also plug your cooker into a kitchen timer that you can set to switch on or off at a designated time, allowing for more peace of mind if you're late getting home. Some models have a Keep Warm setting that the cooker automatically switches to when the allotted cooking time is over. Even so, be sure to practice good food

Size Matters

If you can only buy one slow cooker (and your household consists of more than one person), I recommend you buy a larger model—at least 5½ to 6 quarts. This will allow you more flexibility, plus most of the recipes geared to a 4-quart model can easily be made in a larger one as well, often with no adjustment to the recipe. The larger slow cooker also enables you to make larger-volume recipes, which you can then portion and freeze for further convenience. In addition, certain recipes (such as breads and desserts) call for a pan to be inserted in the cooker, and you will need a larger model to do this. In my house, I regularly use both 4-quart and 6-quart models and sometimes use both sizes at once. Generally, though, the 6-quart gets the most use.

Crockery Care Caveats

- Do not put cold ingredients into a hot slow cooker. It can crack the ceramic insert.

- Let the ceramic insert cool completely before removing and washing it. A sudden change in temperature (such as immersing it in cool dishwater) can crack it.

- Do not immerse the outer electric slow cooker unit in water. Instead, wipe the inside and outside clean with a damp cloth or sponge.

safety: A slow-cooked dish should not be allowed to stand at room temperature for longer than two hours after it is cooked, otherwise you run the risk of harmful bacteria forming.

There are many slow cooker brands available, including the original Crock-Pot made by Rival Manufacturing Company and similar units made by companies such as West Bend, Proctor Silex, and others. In addition, "multi-cookers" are also available, so-named because they can be used for other types of cooking besides slow cooking, such as deep-frying. The multi-cookers have adjustable thermostats that allow you to slow cook on Low (at 200 degrees) or High (300 degrees). However, the multi-cookers are not true slow cookers, because their heating elements are located only in the base of the unit for more direct heat from the bottom, which may result in scorching if the dish is left unattended. In a true slow cooker, the heating elements wrap around in the walls of the appliance, resulting in even, gentle heating. True slow cookers do not have numerical temperature gauges, but rather just Low, High, and Keep Warm settings. The recipes in this book were tested in Rival Crock-Pots, Hamilton Beach/ Proctor Silex Slow Cookers, and West Bend Crockery Cookers.

Volume of Ingredients Versus Size of Slow Cooker

At the beginning of each recipe in this book is a suggested slow cooker size to use for that particular recipe. However, since the amount of the ingredients helps determine the volume, it is important to pay special attention to how full your cooker is after adding the ingredients. For example, if my "small" onion, "large" potato, and so on, are different in size than the ones you are using, you may find that the volume of ingredients in your 3½- or 4-quart cooker is close to full. In some cases, you will need to assess this as you are preparing the recipe. Should you find that you have too many ingredients, you can: a) prepare the recipe in a larger cooker, or b) cut back on the amounts of ingredients you are using. While a slow cooker performs best when at least one-half full but no more than two-thirds full, you can actually make most 3½-

Ten Quick Tips for Slow-Cooking Success

Here are a few simple rules to follow that can make the difference between a so-so meal in your slow cooker and a great one.

1. Do not lift the lid when cooking—it will reduce the cooking temperature considerably and cause your dish to take longer to cook. It is estimated that each time you lift the lid, you lose 20 minutes of cooking time.

2. Always fill your slow cooker at least one-half full. Avoid filling it more than two-thirds full to keep it from spilling over while simmering.

3. As a general rule, the ingredient quantities for a 3½- to 4-quart size slow cooker may be increased by one-half to accommodate a 5½- or 6-quart model, but many recipes contain enough volume to require no adjustment.

4. Note that certain recipes call for partially cooking or browning some of the ingredients before placing them in the slow cooker. The short amount of time this extra step takes can make a world of difference to the taste, texture, and appearance of the dish. In some cases, this step can be done directly in the slow cooker, specifically to soften smaller amounts of vegetables when browning is unnecessary.

5. Some recipes that use quick-cooking or delicate ingredients will call for these ingredients to be added at the end. This attention to detail will pay off when you taste the finished product.

to 4-quart recipes in a 5½- to 6-quart cooker quite successfully. *Be cautioned, however, that if your ingredients come too close to the top (especially when preparing a soup or stew), you run the risk of the contents bubbling up and spilling all over your kitchen counter.* Keep this in mind when assembling ingredients for a recipe, and be aware that you may need to make some adjustments depending on the size of your cooker and the volume of your ingredients.

6. Because the lid remains on throughout most slow-cooked recipes, the liquids do not evaporate the way they do in similar stove-top recipes. Because of this, when converting your own recipes for the slow cooker, you may find that you need to use less liquid when you first put in the ingredients. If you find that you have too much liquid near the end of cooking time, remove the lid and cook on high for an additional 30 to 40 minutes to reduce the excess liquid.

7. Always presoak dried beans. This will help with digestibility and get your slow-cooked beans tender in 8 hours instead of 18.

8. When cooking dried beans, do not add salt, tomatoes, or other acidic ingredients until after the beans have softened, otherwise they will remain somewhat tough. Once the beans are cooked, drain and discard the cooking liquid before using the beans in a recipe. This will also increase digestibility.

9. There are two ways to add pasta or rice to slow-cooked recipes. You can add either uncooked pasta or rice during the final hour of cooking time, or cook the rice or pasta separately and add it to the dish just prior to serving. The latter is my preference, because it gives you more control and assures the proper texture. Rice or pasta cooked directly in the slow cooker often turns out too gummy and starchy. In addition, cooking either ingredient in the cooker will soak up much of the liquid and change the texture of the dish. (Converted rice works best when added raw to a slow cooker recipe. If you prefer brown rice, it's best to cook it separately.)

10. Be sure to read the manufacturer's instructions for cleaning and caring for your slow cooker. Take care of your slow cooker and it will take care of you.

Slow Cooker Recipe Cook Times

When slow cookers first came on the market, the appeal to the working woman was the fact that most recipes listed an eight- to 10-hour cooking time—long enough for the dish to cook all day while she was away at work. While this cooking time may be correct for some recipes, the fact is many of them don't take as long as once thought. In testing the recipes for this book, my testers and I found that many recipes are actually ready to eat much sooner than the traditionally recommended 8 to 10 hours, although some recipes do hold up well when left to cook an additional hour or so. Rather than follow tradition by listing the longest possible cooking time, I felt it important to provide the realistic times when dishes may actually be done while stressing that you can easily tack on an additional hour or so for the food to cook without compromising many of the recipes, and then switch to the Keep Warm setting for a while beyond that. If this still doesn't allow enough time for your recipe to cook while you're away from home, the solution is to purchase an inexpensive kitchen appliance timer to use with your cooker. That way you can assemble your recipe the night before if you wish, refrigerate the insert, then put the insert in the cooker and set the timer to start the cooking up to two hours after you leave the house. That way you can enjoy the convenience of even many of the shorter-cooked recipes if you're away from home all day.

> **High Altitudes**
>
> Those cooking at high elevations (over 3,500 feet) may find that slow-cooked food takes somewhat longer to get done than the cooking times recommended in this cookbook.

Slow Cooker Caveats

The slow cooker is not a magic box—you may think you can just throw in a bunch of ingredients, turn it on, and out comes a fabulous meal. Well, there are certain times when this is true and other times when it isn't. A healthy dose of common sense—and sometimes a little extra effort—can go a long way in successful slow cooker cooking.

In some cases, it may be important to brown or sauté some of the ingredients before adding them to the pot to get the most flavor, a more appealing color, or to jumpstart the cooking process. Onions can be a prime example for all three of these reasons, and you will find that many recipes in this book begin with first cooking onions in a little oil until they soften. It's an extra step worth taking and can be done the night before.

Pot Saver

To save yourself from washing an extra pan, you can soften onions or other hard vegetables directly in the slow cooker. To do this, put oil and hard vegetables in the cooker, cover, and turn on High while you prep the rest of the ingredients. The amount of time this will take depends on the size and volume of the vegetables being used. For example, 1 tablespoon of minced garlic may only take 15 minutes, while ½ cup chopped onion can take up to 30 minutes, so this shortcut is only practical if you plan to be in the kitchen anyway doing other things. If you're in a hurry, you may prefer to opt for the extra dirty pan and sauté your vegetables on top of the stove in five minutes.

On the other hand, certain delicate ingredients are best added near the end of cooking or when you're ready to serve so that their flavors don't dissipate and they don't overcook. Fresh herbs are a good example of ingredients that lose their flavor if added too soon. Cooked pasta or rice should be added near the end of the cooking time so they do not become too soft and mushy.

A Word About Cooking Times

The main reason many of us are enamored with our slow cookers is that they cook dinner while we're out for the day. From that perspective, recipes that take about eight hours to cook will have special appeal. For recipes to finish around the eight-hour mark, they will generally need to be cooked on Low (200°F). If you cook the same recipe on High (300°F), the food will be ready in about half the time. Whenever possible, I cook on Low rather than High, because I think the slower, more gentle cooking coaxes more flavor out of the ingredients. Unless otherwise specified, most recipes in this book use the Low setting, although you may use the High setting if you're pressed for time.

While some recipes require every bit of an eight-hour spread, many recipes will actually be quite ready to eat after about six hours. In such cases, I've listed the cooking time as 6 to 8 hours for those who don't need to use the full 8 hours. Conversely, if you're going to be a little later than eight hours, many recipes will hold over just fine for a little while longer. Some slow cookers have a built-in function that will cook for six or eight hours, for example, then automatically switch to a Keep Warm setting. This kind of cooker is great for people who don't

Extending the Cooking Time

If you're going to be putting in an especially long day at work, the last thing you may feel like doing when you get home is make dinner. Still, many slow cooker recipes are done in 6 to 8 hours and you need it to be more like 10! The solution is as near as your hardware store: plug your cooker into a kitchen timer and you can set it to start up to 2 hours after you leave the house. Another, more low-tech, solution is to prepare your ingredients the night before and place them in the slow cooker insert, then refrigerate it overnight. Before you leave in the morning, place the cold insert in the cooker and turn it on Low. It will take nearly an extra hour for your recipe to cook from the cold state, so you can extend the cooking time that much further. If your cooker has an automatic Keep Warm setting, it will keep your dinner warm for you until you get home. (Remember not to leave food at room temperature for longer than 2 hours.)

arrive home at the same time each day. For food safety reasons, once your food is cooked, you should not let it sit at the Keep Warm setting for longer than two hours. If your schedule requires a longer time frame, I suggest you use a kitchen timer with your cooker and set it to start cooking up to two hours after you leave the house.

Some slow cooker brands and models cook a bit faster (hotter) than others. Therefore, you may need to experiment with the cooking times to your own satisfaction. Other cooking-time variables include the actual temperature of the food you start with (is it at room temperature or cold from the refrigerator?) and the size of the pieces of food being cooked.

If the ingredients in your cooker are cold when you begin cooking, they will take longer than if they were at room temperature. If both the food and slow cooker insert are cold (as would be the case if you assembled your ingredients in the cooker insert the night before and refrigerated it until morning), the cooking time will be longer still. Be sure to factor in some extra time (30 to 45 minutes) for things to warm up when estimating your cooking time.

Vegetarian Ingredients

Since this is a vegetarian cookbook, you won't find the typical slow cooker recipes using cheap cuts of meat. Instead, you will find recipes that use a variety of beans, grains, and vegetables.

In addition, there are recipes that use tofu, tempeh, seitan (also known as "wheat-meat"), and other versatile meat alternatives such as vegetarian burger crumbles and sausage. Here is a brief overview of the meat alternatives used in this book.

Tofu

The first thing to know about tofu is that it comes in different styles. The tofu usually found in the refrigerated case of natural food stores and supermarkets in 16-ounce tubs is referred to as "regular" tofu and also known as "Chinese bean curd." Another kind of tofu, often found in 12-ounce aseptic containers, is known as silken or Japanese-style tofu. Both regular and silken tofu are available in varying textures, from soft to extra firm; the softer the tofu, the more water it contains. Generally speaking, however, silken tofu is softer and creamier than regular tofu.

Because tofu has a delicate texture, it does not generally hold up well in slow cooker recipes unless added right at the end of the cooking time. The kinds of slow cooker recipes most suited to tofu are ones in which the tofu is incorporated into other ingredients, such as terrines, lasagna, stuffings, and desserts. Recipes calling for regular tofu will simply list "tofu" (usually firm or extra-firm). If silken tofu is required, it will be listed as such.

Regular tofu may be stored unopened in the refrigerator until you need it (in accordance with the expiration date on its package). Once tofu is opened, use it as soon as possible. It will keep for 3 to 5 days in the refrigerator if covered in fresh water in a tightly sealed container.

Because tofu is packed in water, it is important to drain it before using, or it may sneak unnoticed moisture into your recipe. After draining the tofu, you should blot it to remove even more moisture. To do this, cut the tofu into slabs and arrange them on a baking pan lined with two or three layers of paper towels. Cover the tofu with additional paper towels and blot. If you wish to remove even more moisture from tofu, you can press it. To do this, follow the steps for blotting tofu, then place a second baking pan on top of the top layer of paper towels. Place some heavy canned goods on top of the pan and allow the tofu to sit for an hour. Removing excess liquid will result in a firmer texture and allow the tofu to better absorb the surrounding flavors in your recipe.

Tempeh

Made from fermented soybeans that are compressed into a cake, tempeh has a chewy, meat-like texture. Because it readily absorbs surrounding flavors, tempeh is especially suited to stews and other slow-cooked recipes. Tempeh can be sliced, diced, cubed, or grated. It is a good idea to sauté it in a little oil before adding it to the slow cooker. It will turn a crisp, golden brown and make the finished dish more visually appealing.

Look for tempeh in the refrigerated or frozen section of natural food stores and larger supermarkets, where it can be found in 8- or 12-ounce packages, depending on the brand. Store tempeh in the refrigerator or freezer. If left unopened, tempeh will keep for several weeks or months (in accordance with the expiration date.) Once opened, it is best to use it within three to four days.

Seitan, or Wheat-Meat

Seitan (say-TAN) is made from the protein part of wheat known as gluten. Seitan's meaty texture and appearance make it a versatile ingredient that is ideal for slow cooking because it absorbs the surrounding flavors as it cooks and its texture holds up during long cooking. You can use diced seitan in stews and soups, shredded or ground seitan in chili, or sliced seitan braised in wine or vegetable stock. Larger pieces can be made into a roast.

Making seitan from scratch (see recipe on page 129) is easy but time-consuming because it needs to be kneaded and rinsed several times before cooking. For that reason, it's best to make a large amount at once and freeze it in usable portions. The seitan-making process requires patience and a bit of faith: During the process, it will look like a gloppy mass of gluten that doesn't stand a chance of holding together, but a minute later it will turn into a firm ball of high-protein wheat gluten. If making homemade seitan does not appeal to you, there is a packaged product called Seitan Quick Mix that combines with water to make fresh seitan without the fuss. Another option is to buy precooked seitan, available in natural food stores and Asian markets. Precooked commercial seitan should be drained and rinsed before using, since it is often sold in a marinade that may not be compatible with your recipe.

Vegetarian Burger Crumbles and Sausage Links

In addition to tofu, tempeh, and seitan, there are many commercial meat alternatives available in the frozen food department of natural food stores and most major supermarkets. These products include vegetarian burgers, sausage links, and burger crumbles that have the flavor and appearance of cooked ground beef. The products are convenient and versatile, with great taste and texture. Because they are precooked, it is best to add them near the end of cooking time in slow cooker recipes. Some ingredients, such as vegetarian sausage links, should be browned in a skillet before using, while others, such as the burger crumbles, do not require browning.

Egg and Dairy Alternatives

To make my recipes accessible to everyone, including vegans, I offer the choice of using alternatives to eggs and dairy products. Some of the ingredients listed include soy milk, soy mozzarella, soy parmesan, and tofu cream cheese. Non-dairy ice cream, such as Tofutti, is a suggested alternative as well. Instead of eggs, I suggest using an egg replacement mixture, a powdered product that is combined with water for use in recipes. The most widely available brand is Ener-G Egg Replacer. Most of these ingredients can be found in well-stocked supermarkets or natural food stores.

Appetizers and Snacks

. . .

Appetizers may not be the first course that comes to mind when you think of slow cooking, but the fact is, slow cookers love a party.

When it comes to entertaining, your slow cooker can help you out in a number of ways. Foremost is that a slow cooker can double as a chafing dish. Just set it out on a buffet table to keep dips and other foods warm throughout the festivities. Also, with the help of a rack or trivet and an inch or two of water, a slow cooker can be used to make pâtés and terrines while your oven is busy doing something else. It's also a practical way to free up a burner when preparing a variety of party foods.

Some of my favorite appetizers, such as dolmas and caponata, benefit from the gentle, scorchless cooking of the slow cooker. In addition, slow cooking is ideal for the preparation of a number of snack foods, including spiced nuts and party mixes, which would otherwise need close attention to keep them from burning.

White Bean and Sun-Dried Tomato Terrine

Serve this terrine with crackers or raw vegetables or spread it on toasted Italian or French bread. If you don't have a trivet that will fit inside your slow cooker, a small heatproof bowl or ramekin will do.

Slow Cooker Size:
6 quart

Cook Time: 4 hours

Setting: Low

Serves 6 to 8

½ cup sun-dried tomatoes
Boiling water as needed
1 tablespoon olive oil
1 small yellow onion, chopped
1 garlic clove, chopped
½ cup blanched whole almonds
3 cups slow-cooked (page 95) or two 15.5-ounce cans cannellini or other white beans, drained and rinsed
2 tablespoons minced fresh parsley leaves
Salt and freshly ground black pepper

1. Place the tomatoes in a heatproof bowl with enough boiling water to cover. Let stand for 30 minutes to soften. Drain, reserving ½ cup of the soaking liquid, and set aside.

2. Heat the oil in a medium-size skillet over medium heat, add the onion and garlic, cover, and cook until softened, about 5 minutes. Set aside.

3. In a food processor, pulse the almonds until coarsely chopped. Add the beans, drained tomatoes, the reserved soaking liquid, onion mixture, and parsley and season with salt and pepper. Process until smooth.

4. Lightly oil a 4-cup terrine mold or a small pan (depending on the shape of your slow cooker). Spoon the mixture inside, pack it in, and smooth the top. Cover with aluminum foil, making several holes in the foil for steam to escape, and place the pan on a rack or trivet that has been set inside a 6-quart slow cooker. Pour an inch of water into the bottom of the cooker. Cover and cook on Low for 4 hours.

5. Remove from the slow cooker and let cool completely before inverting and removing from the mold. Refrigerate for at least several hours or overnight before serving. Serve cool or at room temperature.

Savory Spinach Pâté with Garlic and Pine Nuts

The flavor of this pâté is reminiscent of spanakopita, without the filo pastry. It can be served whole with crackers for spreading or sliced and plated to serve as the first course of a meal.

Slow Cooker Size:
6 quart

Cook Time: 4 hours

Setting: Low

Serves 6 to 8

One 10-ounce package frozen chopped spinach, thawed
1 tablespoon olive oil
2 garlic cloves, chopped
8 ounces extra-firm tofu, well drained
1½ cups slow-cooked (page 95) or one 15.5-ounce can cannellini or other white beans, drained and rinsed
½ cup pine nuts, toasted (see sidebar) and coarsely chopped
1 tablespoon fresh lemon juice
1 teaspoon dillweed, crumbled
Salt and freshly ground black pepper

How to Toast Pine Nuts

Place the pine nuts in a dry skillet over medium heat, shaking or stirring constantly until toasted to a light golden brown. Remove from the hot pan immediately or they will continue to darken.

1. Cook the spinach according to the package directions. Drain very well to remove excess water from the spinach, squeeze dry in a clean dish towel, and set aside.

2. Heat the oil in a medium-size skillet over medium heat, add the garlic, and cook, stirring, until fragrant, about 30 seconds. Add the spinach and cook until any remaining moisture evaporates.

3. In a food processor, combine the spinach mixture, tofu, beans, pine nuts, lemon juice, dillweed, and salt and pepper to taste, and process until smooth.

4. Lightly oil a small loaf pan or 7-inch springform pan (depending on the shape of your slow cooker). Spoon the pâté mixture inside, pack it in, and smooth the top. Cover with aluminum foil, making several holes in the foil for steam to escape. Place the pan on a rack or trivet that has been set inside a 6-quart slow cooker. Pour an inch of water into the bottom of the cooker. Cover and cook on Low for 4 hours.

5. Remove from the slow cooker and let cool completely before removing from pan. Refrigerate for at least several hours or overnight before serving. Serve cool or at room temperature.

Vegetarian Country-Style Pâté

I like the hearty flavor of this country-style pâté made with eggplant, lentils, walnuts, and tofu. The flavor improves if you make it ahead and refrigerate it overnight.

Slow Cooker Size: 6 quart

Cook Time: 4 hours

Setting: Low

Serves 6 to 8

1 medium-size eggplant, peeled and sliced
1 tablespoon olive oil
1 small yellow onion, chopped
2 garlic cloves, minced
2 cups cooked brown lentils, well drained
1 cup finely ground walnuts
⅓ cup tahini
1 cup drained firm tofu
2 tablespoons tamari or other soy sauce
2 tablespoons chopped fresh parsley leaves
1 teaspoon dried thyme
1 teaspoon sweet paprika
¼ teaspoon ground allspice
⅛ teaspoon cayenne pepper
Salt and freshly ground black pepper
2 tablespoons all-purpose flour

1. Preheat the oven to 375°F. Place the eggplant on a lightly oiled baking pan and bake until soft, turning once, about 20 minutes. Set aside to cool.

2. Heat the oil in a small skillet over medium heat, add the onion and garlic, cover, and cook, stirring, until softened, about 5 minutes.

3. Place the onion mixture in a food processor along with the eggplant. Add the remaining ingredients, except the flour, and process until just combined. Do not overprocess. Taste and adjust the seasonings. Stir in the flour.

4. Lightly oil a small loaf pan or 7-inch springform pan, depending on the shape of your slow cooker. Fill with the pâté mixture, packing it in and smoothing the top. Cover with aluminum foil, making several holes in the foil for steam to escape and place the pan on a trivet or rack that has been set inside a 6-quart slow cooker. Pour an inch of water into the bottom of the cooker. Cover and cook on Low for 4 hours.

5. Remove from the slow cooker and let cool completely before removing from the pan. Refrigerate for at least several hours or overnight before serving.

Chutney-Topped Tofu Appetizer Cheesecake

This savory spread was inspired by a baked brie appetizer topped with chutney that I served during my catering days. It looks great on the buffet table and is best served with light, crisp crackers.

Slow Cooker Size: 6 quart

Cook Time: 4 hours

Setting: Low

Serves 12

1 cup unsalted raw cashews, finely ground
One 8-ounce package regular or tofu cream cheese
One 8-ounce package silken tofu
1 tablespoon cornstarch
1 tablespoon curry powder
1 teaspoon salt
¼ teaspoon cayenne pepper
1 cup mango chutney

1. Preheat the oven to 400°F. Lightly oil the inside of a 7-inch springform pan. Spread the ground cashews over the bottom of the pan and use your hands to press them into an even layer. Place the pan in the oven until cashew crust is lightly toasted, about 5 minutes. Be careful not to burn the nuts. Remove from the oven and set aside.

2. In a food processor or using a hand mixer, process or beat the cream cheese until smooth. Add the tofu, cornstarch, curry powder, salt, and cayenne, and blend until smooth. Pour the mixture evenly into the prepared pan. Cover with aluminum foil, making several holes in the foil for steam to escape. Place a trivet, rack, or small heatproof bowl in the bottom of a 6-quart slow cooker. Pour an inch of boiling water into the bottom of the cooker. Place the foil-covered springform pan on top of the trivet, cover and cook on Low for 4 hours.

3. Take the pan out of the cooker, remove the foil, and let it stand until cool. Once cool, cover, and refrigerate for at least several hours or overnight. Let cool completely before removing from the pan.

4. To serve, remove the sides of the pan, using a knife to loosen it if necessary. Spread the top of the cheesecake with the chutney and serve.

Thyme-Scented Duxelles Crostini

The first time I made duxelles—a slowly cooked mixture of mushrooms, shallots, and herbs—I wondered if all that stirring would be worth the trouble; after all, it was only mushrooms. Once I had my first taste, however, I was hooked. When you make them in a slow cooker, you have the best of both worlds—great tasting duxelles and the freedom to do something else while the mushrooms gently cook unattended. If you don't use all the duxelles for crostini, use the rest in sauces, stews, or stuffings or to make a great mushroom risotto. Properly stored in an airtight container in the refrigerator, the duxelles mixture will keep for up to a week.

Slow Cooker Size:
4 quart

Cook Time: 6 to 8 hours

Setting: Low

Makes about
2½ cups

¼ cup olive oil

3 medium-size shallots, minced

2 pounds white mushrooms, stems trimmed and wiped clean

2 teaspoons minced fresh thyme leaves or 1 teaspoon dried

½ teaspoon salt

Freshly ground black pepper

¼ cup regular or tofu cream cheese

3 tablespoons dry white wine

1 loaf French bread, cut into rounds and toasted

1. Place the oil and shallots in a 4-quart slow cooker. Cover and turn the setting to High to soften the shallots while you prepare the mushrooms.

2. Using a food processor or by hand, coarsely chop the mushrooms. Add them to the slow cooker and change the setting to Low. Cover and cook until the mushrooms are very soft, 6 to 8 hours.

3. After the mushrooms are cooked, strain the excess mushroom liquid into a bowl and reserve for use in another recipe.

4. Transfer the mushroom mixture to a food processor, add the thyme, salt, and pepper, and pulse to combine. Add the cream cheese and wine and process until blended. Taste to adjust the seasonings.

5. When ready to serve, spread the duxelles mixture onto the toasted bread rounds. Alternatively, you may put the duxelles mixture in a bowl and allow guests to spread it on the toasted bread themselves.

Slow Stuffed Grape Leaves

Traditionally known as *dolmas*, these tiny bundles are made with grape leaves, which can be found in specialty food shops and well-stocked supermarkets. *Dolmas* prepared using the conventional stove-top method are subject to scorching, but the slow cooker eliminates that problem.

Slow Cooker Size:
3½ to 4 quart

Cook Time: 4 to 6 hours

Setting: Low

Makes about 24

One 16-ounce jar grape leaves, drained
2 tablespoons olive oil
1 small yellow onion, minced
¾ cup raw basmati rice
¼ cup pine nuts, toasted (page 16)
½ teaspoon ground allspice
2 cups vegetable stock (see A Note About Stock, page 32)
Salt and freshly ground black pepper
2 tablespoons minced fresh parsley leaves
1 tablespoon fresh lemon juice

1. Rinse the grape leaves under running water, then pat dry and trim off the stems. Set aside.

2. Heat 1 tablespoon of the oil in a large skillet over medium heat. Add the onion, cover, and cook until softened, about 5 minutes. Stir in the rice, pine nuts, allspice, and 1 cup of stock, season with salt and pepper, cover, and simmer until the liquid is evaporated and the rice is just tender, stirring occasionally, about 20 minutes. Transfer the filling to a bowl, stir in the parsley, and set aside to cool.

3. Place a grape leaf on a flat work surface, shiny side down, pointing the stem end toward you. Place 1 tablespoon of the rice mixture near the stem end and fold in the sides of the leaf over the filling. Roll the leaf away from you, firmly but not too tightly. Repeat until all the leaves and filling are used.

4. Transfer the stuffed grape leaves to a 3½- to 4-quart slow cooker, arranging them in layers. Pour the remaining 1 cup stock, 1 tablespoon olive oil, and the lemon juice over the stuffed leaves. Add a small amount of water, if necessary, so that all the *dolmas* are just covered with liquid. Cover and cook on Low for 4 to 6 hours.

5. Uncover and allow to cool, then drain the liquid and transfer the stuffed grape leaves to a serving plate. Serve at room temperature.

Caponata

This sweet-and-sour eggplant mélange has its roots in Southern Italy. It can be enjoyed as a side dish or as part of an antipasto platter. Best served at room temperature, caponata is also terrific spooned onto crackers, as a crostini topping, or even served over pasta. Make the caponata at least a few hours ahead of time or the day before so the flavors have a chance to blend before serving.

Slow Cooker Size:
4 quart

Cook Time: 6 hours

Setting: Low

Serves 6

2 tablespoons olive oil
1 medium-size yellow onion, chopped
1 celery rib, minced
1 large eggplant, peeled and diced
1 medium-size red or green bell pepper, seeded and chopped
3 garlic cloves, minced
One 14.5-ounce can diced tomatoes, drained and chopped
1 tablespoon tomato paste
2 tablespoons red wine vinegar
1 tablespoon sugar
½ teaspoon dried basil
¼ teaspoon dried oregano
¼ teaspoon red pepper flakes, or to taste
Salt and freshly ground black pepper
⅓ cup black olives, drained, pitted, and sliced
1 tablespoon capers, drained and chopped
1 tablespoon minced fresh parsley leaves

1. Heat the oil in a large skillet over medium heat. Add the onion and celery, cover, and cook until softened, about 5 minutes. Add the eggplant, cover, and cook, stirring occasionally, until the eggplant begins to soften, about 5 more minutes.

2. Transfer the mixture to a 4-quart slow cooker. Add the bell pepper, garlic, tomatoes, tomato paste, vinegar, sugar, basil, oregano, and red pepper flakes, and season with salt and pepper. Cover and cook on Low until the vegetables are soft but still hold some shape, about 6 hours.

3. When the vegetables are cooked, stir in the olives, capers, and parsley. Taste to adjust the seasonings. Transfer the caponata to a bowl and let cool. Serve at room temperature. If not serving right away, cover and refrigerate until needed.

Tempeh and Shallot Confit

A confit is traditionally made with ingredients that are slow-cooked in animal fat. This version uses olive oil to slow-cook tempeh and shallots. Because of its hearty, intense flavor, a little goes a long way. Serve spread on crackers or toasted bread rounds or use to enrich the Slow and Easy White Bean Cassoulet on page 102.

Slow Cooker Size:
1 to 1½ quart

Cook Time: 4 hours

Setting: Low

Makes about 2 cups

¼ cup olive oil
4 shallots, thinly sliced
8 ounces tempeh, coarsely chopped
2 tablespoons cider vinegar
2 tablespoons packed light brown sugar or a natural sweetener
Salt and freshly ground black pepper

1. Heat 2 tablespoons of the oil in a medium-size skillet over medium heat. Add the shallots, cover, and cook until softened, about 5 minutes.

2. Transfer the shallots to the insert of a 1- to 1½-quart slow cooker and turn it on High. Add the remaining oil, the tempeh, vinegar, and brown sugar; season with salt and pepper, cover, and cook on Low until the mixture becomes thick and syrupy, about 4 hours.

3. Transfer to a bowl to cool. Serve cool or at room temperature. Refrigerate unused confit in a tightly covered container.

Note: Because of the small volume in this recipe, a 1- to 1½-quart slow cooker is recommended.

Spicy Chili Dip

This easy dip is great for casual gatherings and, best of all, you can make and serve it in the slow cooker, where it will stay warm for hours without burning.

Slow Cooker Size:
1 to 1½ quart

Cook Time: 2 hours

Setting: Low

Makes about 3½ cups

2 cups frozen vegetarian burger crumbles or 3 frozen veggie burgers, thawed and crumbled or chopped

¾ cup salsa of your choice

1 tablespoon chili powder

¼ teaspoon cayenne pepper

½ cup shredded cheddar cheese or soy cheddar

Salt

3 tablespoons canned diced green chiles

3 tablespoons sliced black olives

Tortilla chips

1. Place the crumbles, salsa, chili powder, cayenne, cheese, and salt in a 1- to 1½-quart slow cooker and stir to combine. Cover and cook on Low for 2 hours.

2. Just before serving, remove the lid and top with the chiles and olives. Serve warm with tortilla chips.

Note: Because of the small volume in this recipe, a 1- to 1½-quart slow cooker is recommended.

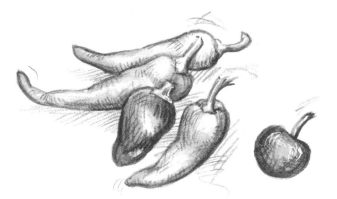

Artichoke Dip with a Kick

A generous splash of Tabasco adds a bit of heat to the usually mild-mannered artichoke dip. This version uses both plain and marinated artichoke hearts for a balanced flavor. Serve directly from the slow cooker, with the temperature setting on Low to keep it at serving temperature for several hours. Accompany with crackers or lightly toasted French bread rounds.

Slow Cooker Size:
1 to 1½ quart

Cook Time: 2 hours

Setting: Low

Makes about
3½ cups

One 9-ounce package frozen artichoke hearts, cooked according to package directions and drained
One 8-ounce jar marinated artichoke hearts, drained and chopped
One 8-ounce package regular or tofu cream cheese, at room temperature
4 scallions, minced
½ cup freshly grated Parmesan cheese or soy Parmesan
1 tablespoon fresh lemon juice
½ teaspoon Tabasco sauce, or to taste
Salt

1. Coarsely chop all the artichoke hearts, then place them in a medium-size bowl. Add the cream cheese, scallions, Parmesan, lemon juice, and Tabasco and season with salt. Mix well.

2. Lightly oil the insert of a 1- to 1½-quart slow cooker and spoon the artichoke mixture inside, spreading it evenly. Cover and cook on Low for 2 hours.

Note: Because of the small volume in this recipe, a 1- to 1½-quart slow cooker is recommended.

Ragin' Cajun Pecans

Keep some of these yummy nuts on hand for when guests drop by—they're especially good served with cold beer. If you prefer them less spicy, cut back on the chili powder and cayenne.

Slow Cooker Size:
3½ to 4 quart

Cook Time: 2¾ hours

Setting: 15 minutes on High; 2½ hours on Low

Makes about 4 cups

1 pound unsalted raw pecan halves (about 4 cups)
¼ cup olive oil
1 tablespoon chili powder
1 teaspoon dried thyme
1 teaspoon salt
½ teaspoon dried oregano
½ teaspoon onion powder
¼ teaspoon garlic powder
¼ teaspoon celery salt
¼ teaspoon cayenne pepper

1. Combine the pecans and oil in a 3½- to 4-quart slow cooker, stirring to coat. Cover and cook on High for 15 minutes.

2. In a small bowl, combine the herbs and spices. Remove the cooker cover, adjust the setting to Low, and sprinkle the mixture over the pecans, stirring to coat them evenly with it. Cook, uncovered, stirring occasionally, for 2½ hours.

3. Spread the nuts in a single layer on a baking sheet and let cool completely. When cool, the nuts may be stored in airtight container in the refrigerator until ready to use. Serve warm or at room temperature. Properly stored, the pecans will keep in the refrigerator for up to 4 weeks or in the freezer for 2 to 3 months.

Ginger-Spiced Walnuts

I like to keep these on hand to serve during the holidays. They also make nice gifts when put in jars and decorated with ribbon. Crystallized ginger comes sold in small pieces. Use a spice grinder to grind it into a powder.

Slow Cooker Size:
3½ to 4 quart

Cook Time: 2¼ hours

Setting: 15 minutes on High; 2 hours on Low

Makes about 4 cups

1 pound unsalted raw walnut halves (about 4 cups)
¼ cup corn oil or other mild-tasting oil
⅓ cup packed light brown sugar
1 tablespoon ground crystallized ginger
1 teaspoon ground cinnamon
½ teaspoon ground allspice

1. Combine the walnuts and oil in a 3½- to 4-quart slow cooker, stirring to coat. Add the brown sugar, stirring to coat evenly. Cover and cook on High for 15 minutes. Adjust the setting to Low and cook, uncovered, stirring occasionally, until the nuts are coated with a crisp glaze, about 2 hours.

2. In a small bowl, combine the ginger, cinnamon, and allspice and sprinkle over the nuts, stirring to coat evenly. Spread the nuts out in a single layer on a baking sheet and let cool completely before serving. These nuts will keep in the refrigerator, tightly covered, for up to a month or in the freezer for 2 to 3 months.

Tamari Almonds

These are less expensive than the kind you buy in stores, and you can reduce the sodium content by using a low-sodium tamari.

Slow Cooker Size:
3½ to 4 quart

Cook Time: 2¾ hours

Setting: 15 minutes on High; 2½ hours on Low

Makes about 4 cups

1 pound unsalted raw whole almonds (about 4 cups)
3 tablespoons peanut oil
3 tablespoons tamari soy sauce
⅛ teaspoon cayenne pepper

1. Combine all the ingredients in a 3½- to 4-quart slow cooker, stirring to coat. Cover and cook on High for 15 minutes. Remove the cover, adjust the setting to Low, and cook, uncovered, stirring occasionally, for 2½ hours.

2. Spread the nuts out in a single layer on a baking sheet and let them cool completely. When cool, the nuts may be stored in airtight container in the refrigerator until ready to use. Serve warm or at room temperature. Properly stored, the almonds will keep in the refrigerator for up to 4 weeks or in the freezer for 2 to 3 months.

Santa Fe Trail Mix

Try this Southwestern version of everyone's favorite party mix at your next casual get-together. Use either garlic salt or celery salt according to your personal preference—you can even add some of each, if you like.

Slow Cooker Size:
3½ to 4 quart

Cook Time: 3 hours

Setting: Low

Makes about
8½ cups

2 cups small corn chips (like Fritos)
2 cups roasted unsalted peanuts
2 cups thin pretzel sticks
1½ cups crispy corn cereal squares
1 cup pepitas (pumpkin seeds)
⅓ cup corn oil
¼ cup packed light brown sugar
2 tablespoons tamari or other soy sauce
1 tablespoon chili powder, or to tase
1 teaspoon garlic salt or celery salt, or to taste

1. In a large bowl, combine the corn chips, peanuts, pretzels, cereal, and pumpkin seeds.

2. In a separate bowl, whisk together the oil, brown sugar, tamari, chili powder, and garlic salt. Pour the wet mixture over the dry mixture, stirring gently to coat evenly.

3. Transfer the mixture to a 3½- to 4-quart slow cooker and cook, uncovered, on Low, stirring occasionally, for 3 hours.

4. Spread the mixture out in a single layer on a baking sheet and let cool completely. Store in an airtight container until ready to use. Properly stored, this will keep for several weeks.

Asian-Style Party Mix

Asian rice crackers, roasted peas, and nori (the sea vegetable used to make sushi) are available in Asian markets, natural food stores, and well-stocked supermarkets.

Slow Cooker Size:
3½ to 4 quart

Cook Time: 3 hours

Setting: Low

Makes about
8½ cups

3 cups crispy rice cereal squares
2 cups small Asian rice crackers
2 cups roasted soy nuts
1½ cups roasted peas (plain or wasabi-flavored)
2 tablespoons sesame seeds
½ cup brown rice syrup
¼ cup toasted sesame oil
2 tablespoons peanut oil
2 tablespoons tamari or other soy sauce
2 tablespoons packed light brown sugar
1 sheet nori

1. In a large bowl, combine the cereal, crackers, soy nuts, peas, and sesame seeds.

2. In a medium-size saucepan, combine the brown rice syrup, oils, tamari, and brown sugar and cook over medium heat, stirring, until hot and the brown sugar has dissolved, about 5 minutes. Pour the wet mixture over the dry ingredients in the bowl, stirring gently to combine.

3. Transfer the mixture to a 3½ - to 4-quart slow cooker and cook, uncovered, on Low for 3 hours, stirring occasionally.

4. Spread the mixture in a single layer on a baking sheet and let cool completely. Store in an airtight container until ready to use. Properly stored, this will keep for several weeks.

5. Just before serving, use a pair of scissors to cut the nori into 1-inch-long strips and cut the strips into ¼-inch-wide lengths. Stir the nori into the mix and serve. Once the mix contains the nori strips, it should be used within a few hours.

Soups and Chowders

. . .

Thanks to the slow cooker, homemade soup doesn't have to be just a memory of something your grandmother made. Even those of us with busy schedules and hectic lifestyles can enjoy the simple pleasure of a bowl of hot, freshly made soup.

Soups and slow cookers are a perfect match—just combine your ingredients, turn on the cooker, and don't think about it again until dinnertime. That's when you get to ladle out the rich broth and fresh ingredients that taste like you spent all day cooking.

Soups are perhaps the most forgiving of slow-cooked recipes. You can add, increase, or delete certain ingredients to your own taste, and chances are the soup will still turn out fine. In addition, even when you leave most soups cooking (or keeping warm) beyond when they're "done," they still hold up well. Most soups (and stews) do best in a 5½- or 6-quart slow cooker because they need a few inches of "head room" so they can bubble up when simmering without spilling over. In addition, the size variation in certain ingredients may affect the volume of what goes into your cooker, and a larger model is better able to handle such discrepancies.

Use your slow cooker to try the wholesome soups in this chapter, which begins with two great vegetable stocks and moves on to lots of hearty bean soups and a variety of vegetable soups. There are even dairy-free versions of cream soups made silken with potatoes, beans, and vegetable purées—so smooth and delicious, you'll never miss the cream—or the calories.

A Note about Stock

When a recipe calls for vegetable stock, you have several options. First, you can use homemade stock by whipping up either of the vegetable stock recipes that follow—Light and Easy Vegetable Stock (page 34) or Vegetable Super-Stock (page 35). Alternatively, there are several brands of commercial vegetable broth available that can be used instead. A third option is to use water boosted with a proportionate amount of powdered vegetable base. Because these choices will vary in degree of saltiness, you will find that most recipes using vegetable stock will also call for salt "to taste" so that you can make adjustments accordingly.

Light and Easy Vegetable Stock

This stock is so simple to make that it will be a cinch to keep some on hand to enrich your soups, stews, and other recipes. A $5\frac{1}{2}$- to 6-quart cooker is best to allow enough space for the stock to simmer. If using a smaller cooker, you may need to cut back slightly on the amounts of the ingredients.

Slow Cooker Size:
4 to 6 quart

Cook Time: 8 to 10 hours

Setting: Low

Makes about 8 cups

1 tablespoon olive oil
2 medium-size yellow onions, quartered
2 large carrots, cut into 1-inch pieces
1 celery rib, cut into 1-inch pieces
2 or 3 garlic cloves, left unpeeled and crushed
Peels from 2 large well-scrubbed potatoes
$\frac{1}{3}$ cup coarsely chopped fresh parsley leaves
1 large bay leaf
$\frac{1}{2}$ teaspoon black peppercorns
8 cups water
2 teaspoons tamari or other soy sauce
1 teaspoon salt

1. Drizzle the oil in the bottom of a 4- to 6-quart slow cooker. Add the onions, carrots, celery, garlic, potato peels, parsley, bay leaf, and peppercorns, pour in the water, and add the tamari and salt. Cover and cook on Low for 8 to 10 hours.

2. Allow the stock to cool slightly, then strain it through a fine-mesh sieve into a pot or bowl, pressing the vegetables against the sieve to release all the juices. Store the cooled stock in tightly sealed containers where it will keep for 3 to 5 days in the refrigerator or in the freezer for up to 3 months.

Vegetable Super-Stock

Although this stock takes a little extra work, it rewards you by tasting extra good. The full-bodied flavor and rich color comes from roasting the vegetables before adding them to the slow cooker.

Slow Cooker Size:
4 to 6 quart

Cook Time: 8 hours

Setting: Low

Makes about 8 cups

1 large yellow onion, thickly sliced
2 large carrots, cut into 1-inch chunks
1 large all-purpose potato, left unpeeled and cut into 1-inch chunks
1 large parsnip, peeled and cut into 1-inch chunks
1 celery rib, cut into 1-inch pieces
3 garlic cloves, left unpeeled and crushed
1 tablespoon olive oil
Salt and freshly ground black pepper
½ cup coarsely chopped fresh parsley leaves
4 dried shiitake or porcini mushrooms, soaked in 1 cup hot water until softened, drained, and soaking liquid strained of grit and reserved
2 bay leaves
½ teaspoon black peppercorns
1 tablespoon tamari or other soy sauce
7 cups water

1. Preheat the oven to 450°F. Place the onion, carrots, potato, parsnip, celery, and garlic in a lightly oiled baking pan. Drizzle with the oil and sprinkle with salt and pepper. Roast the vegetables until slightly browned, turning once, about 30 minutes total.

2. Transfer the roasted vegetables to a 4- to 6-quart slow cooker. Add the parsley, mushrooms and their soaking water, bay leaves, peppercorns, tamari, 1 teaspoon salt, and the water. Cover and cook on Low for 8 hours, until the vegetables are soft and the stock is a rich golden color.

3. Let the stock cool slightly, then strain through a fine-mesh sieve into a large bowl or pot, pressing against the solids with the back of a spoon to release the liquid. Use at once or let cool completely, then portion and store in the refrigerator in tightly covered containers. Properly stored, the stock will keep in the refrigerator for up to 5 days or in the freezer up to 3 months.

Black Bean Soup

In addition to thickening the soup, puréeing some of the some solids, as you do in this soup, gives it added flavor and a creamier texture.

Slow Cooker Size:
4 to 6 quart

Cook Time: 8 hours

Setting: Low

Serves 4 to 6

1 tablespoon olive oil
1 medium-size yellow onion, chopped
1 medium-size carrot, chopped
½ small green bell pepper, seeded and minced
2 garlic cloves, minced
3 cups slow-cooked (page 95) or two 15.5-ounce cans black beans, drained and rinsed
One 14.5-ounce can diced tomatoes, left undrained
4 cups vegetable stock (see A Note About Stock, page 32)
2 bay leaves
1 teaspoon ground cumin
1 teaspoon dried thyme
¼ teaspoon cayenne pepper
Salt and freshly ground black pepper
2 teaspoons fresh lemon juice (optional)

1. Heat the oil in a large skillet over medium heat. Add the onion, carrot, bell pepper, and garlic, cover, and cook until softened, about 5 minutes.

2. Transfer the cooked vegetables to a 4- to 6-quart slow cooker, add the beans, tomatoes and their juice, stock, bay leaves, cumin, thyme, and cayenne, and season with salt and black pepper. Stir to combine. Cover and cook on Low for 8 hours.

3. Remove and discard the bay leaf and taste to adjust the seasonings. Just before serving, stir in the lemon juice, if using. To thicken, purée at least 2 cups or up to one half of the soup solids with an immersion blender used right in the cooker, or ladled into a regular blender or food processor and returned to the cooker. Serve hot.

Tuscan White Bean and Escarole Soup

Soothing and delicious, this soup has a restorative quality that seems to revive me right from the first spoonful. Escarole is too bitter to cook directly in the soup, so it will need to be cooked separately and added when ready to serve. At the same time, you can cook up a small amount of pasta to add to the soup, though, if you prefer, you can add the raw pasta directly to the soup about 1 hour before the soup is ready to serve. I find it easiest to cook the escarole and pasta ahead of time to add to the soup when I'm ready to serve it.

Slow Cooker Size:
4 to 6 quart

Cook Time: 6 to 8 hours
(pasta added during
last hour of cooking)

Setting: Low

Serves 6

1 tablespoon olive oil
1 medium-size yellow onion, minced
3 large garlic cloves, minced
3 cups slow-cooked (page 95) or two 15.5-ounce cans cannellini or
   other white beans, drained and rinsed
6 cups vegetable stock (see A Note About Stock, page 32)
¼ teaspoon red pepper flakes, or to taste
Salt and freshly ground black pepper
1 small head escarole, coarsely chopped
½ cup *ditalini* or other small pasta shape

1. Heat the oil in a large saucepan over medium heat. Add the onion, cover, and cook until softened, about 5 minutes. Add the garlic and cook 1 minute.

2. Transfer the onion and garlic to a 4- to 6-quart quart slow cooker. Add the beans, stock, and red pepper flakes and season with salt and black pepper. Cover and cook on Low for 6 to 8 hours.

3. Cook the escarole in a pot of boiling salted water until softened, about 5 minutes. Drain and set aside. In a small saucepan of boiling salted water, cook the *ditalini* until *al dente*, about 5 minutes. Drain and add to the soup, along with the cooked escarole, just before serving.

French White Bean and Cabbage Soup

Similar to the Tuscan soup called *ribollita*, this country French soup is "peasant food" at its best. Known as *garbure* in France, it traditionally uses goose confit and pork, but slow cooking provides this vegetarian version with plenty of rich flavor without the meat. However, if you do want to add a "meaty" flavor, you can brown vegetarian sausage links cut into 1-inch pieces and add them to the soup at serving time or spoon in some Tempeh and Shallot Confit (page 22). Crusty French bread is a natural accompaniment.

I use a 6-quart slow cooker for this soup, since the large amount of ingredients can crowd a smaller cooker. If you only have a 3½- or 4-quart cooker, simply cut back slightly on the ingredient amounts as needed so as to not overfill it.

Slow Cooker Size: 6 quart	2 tablespoons olive oil
	1 medium-size yellow onion, chopped
Cook Time: 8 hours	1 medium-size carrot, chopped
	3 garlic cloves, minced
Setting: Low	1 small head green cabbage, cored and shredded
	1 large Yukon Gold potato, peeled and diced
Serves 6	1½ cups slow-cooked (page 95) or one 15.5-ounce can cannellini or other white beans, drained and rinsed

2 tablespoons olive oil
1 medium-size yellow onion, chopped
1 medium-size carrot, chopped
3 garlic cloves, minced
1 small head green cabbage, cored and shredded
1 large Yukon Gold potato, peeled and diced
1½ cups slow-cooked (page 95) or one 15.5-ounce can cannellini or other white beans, drained and rinsed
6 cups vegetable stock (see A Note About Stock, page 32)
¾ teaspoon dried thyme
Salt and freshly ground black pepper
1 teaspoon Liquid Smoke (optional)
1 tablespoon minced fresh parsley leaves

1. Heat the oil in a large saucepan over medium heat. Add the onion, carrot, and garlic, cover, and cook until softened, about 5 minutes.

2. Transfer the cooked vegetables to a 6-quart slow cooker. Add the cabbage, potato, beans, stock, and thyme; season with salt and pepper, cover, and cook on Low for 8 hours.

3. Just before serving, stir in the Liquid Smoke, if using, and parsley. Taste to adjust the seasonings.

Lentil Soup with Ribbons of Kale

Collards, chard, or other dark greens may be substituted for the kale. I prefer to cook the greens in advance and add them when the soup is ready to eat, because cooking the raw greens right in the soup can impart a bitter flavor.

Slow Cooker Size:
4 to 6 quart

Cook Time: 8 hours

Setting: Low

Serves 6

1 tablespoon olive oil
1 large yellow onion, chopped
1 celery rib, chopped
1 large carrot, chopped
2 garlic cloves, minced
1¼ cups dried brown lentils, picked over and rinsed
6 cups vegetable stock (see A Note About Stock, page 32) or water
1 tablespoon tamari or other soy sauce
Salt and freshly ground black pepper
4 or 5 large kale leaves, tough stems removed

1. Heat the oil in a large saucepan over medium heat. Add the onion, celery, carrot, and garlic, cover, and cook until softened, 8 to 10 minutes.

2. Transfer the cooked vegetables to a 4- to 6-quart slow cooker, add the lentils, stock, and tamari; cover, and cook on Low for 8 hours. Season with salt and pepper.

3. Meanwhile, or beforehand, tightly roll the kale leaves up like a cigar and cut them crosswise into thin ribbons. Cook the kale in a pot of boiling salted water until tender, about 5 minutes, and add to the soup when ready to serve.

Moroccan-Style Lentil and Chickpea Soup

Inspired by *harira*, the classic bean and vegetable soup of Morocco, this thick and spicy soup is especially delicious when left to simmer all day in a slow cooker.

Slow Cooker Size:
4 to 6 quart

Cook Time: 8 hours

Setting: Low

Serves 6

1 tablespoon olive oil

1 medium-size yellow onion, chopped

1 small carrot, chopped

3 garlic cloves, chopped

½ teaspoon peeled and minced fresh ginger

½ teaspoon turmeric

½ teaspoon ground cinnamon

¼ teaspoon ground cumin

¼ teaspoon ground cardamom

½ cup dried lentils, picked over and rinsed

One 14.5-ounce can plum tomatoes, drained and chopped

1½ cups slow-cooked (page 95) or one 15.5-ounce can chickpeas, drained and rinsed

6 cups vegetable stock (see A Note About Stock, page 32)

1 tablespoon fresh lemon juice

1 to 2 teaspoons harissa sauce, to taste, plus more to serve (recipe follows)

Salt and freshly ground black pepper

1. Heat the oil in a large skillet over medium heat. Add the onion, carrot, and garlic, cover, and cook until slightly softened, about 5 minutes. Add the ginger, turmeric, cinnamon, cumin, and cardamom, stirring to coat the vegetables.

2. Transfer the onion mixture to a 4- to 6-quart slow cooker, add the lentils, tomatoes, chickpeas, and stock, cover, and cook on Low for 8 hours.

3. About 10 minutes before serving, add the lemon juice and harissa and season with salt and pepper. A small bowl of harissa may be placed on the table for those who wish to add more.

Harissa Sauce

In addition to using this spicy condiment in the Moroccan soup, it can also be used to spice up other soups, as well as stews and grilled vegetables. Mild chiles, such as ancho, may be used instead of hot ones if you prefer. Harissa sauce can also be purchased ready-made in Middle Eastern and specialty food stores.

4 dried red chiles, stemmed and seeded
2 large garlic cloves, peeled
1 tablespoon olive oil
¾ teaspoon ground caraway seeds
¾ teaspoon ground coriander
½ teaspoon salt
3 tablespoons water

1. Break the chiles into pieces and place in a heatproof bowl. Add enough boiling water to cover and let soak for 5 minutes.

2. Drain the chiles and place them in a food processor. Add the garlic, oil, caraway, coriander, and salt and process until puréed. Add the water and process until smooth. Transfer the sauce to a tightly covered container and store in the refrigerator until ready to use. Properly stored, it will keep for several weeks.

Makes about ½ cup

Split Pea and Parsnip Soup

The parsnips add a creamy sweetness that complements the flavor of the split peas. If parsnips are unavailable, use carrots instead. Because the peas have a tendency to settle on the bottom of the pot, a quick stir midway through the cooking process is helpful. The amount of salt you need will depend on the saltiness of the stock you are using—usually about 1 teaspoon is a good place to start. The Liquid Smoke adds a "bacony" flavor to the soup; it is available in well-stocked supermarkets.

Slow Cooker Size:
4 to 6 quart

Cook Time: 8 hours

Setting: Low

Serves 4 to 6

1 tablespoon olive oil

1 medium-size yellow onion, chopped

2 large parsnips, peeled, halved lengthwise, and cut into thin half moons

1 pound dried green split peas, picked over and rinsed

1 teaspoon dried thyme

1 bay leaf

6 cups vegetable stock (see A Note About Stock, page 32)

1 teaspoon salt, or to taste

Freshly ground black pepper

1 teaspoon Liquid Smoke (optional)

1. Heat the oil in a large skillet over medium heat, add the onion and parsnips, cover, and cook until softened, about 5 minutes.

2. Transfer the vegetables to a 4- to 6-quart slow cooker and add the peas, thyme, bay leaf, and stock. Cover and cook on Low for 8 hours, stirring once during the cooking process, if possible.

3. Season with the salt and pepper to taste. Stir in the Liquid Smoke, if using, remove and discard the bay leaf, and taste to adjust the seasonings.

Very Vegetable Gumbo

Cajun gumbo has become a favorite across the nation. Many versions exist, and now you can add one more to your gumbo repertoire: a slow-simmered okra-free gumbo that adds zucchini to the list of vegetables simmering in the flavorful broth. Filé powder, available in well-stocked supermarkets and gourmet grocers, is made from ground sassafras leaves and lends thickness and flavor to the gumbo, while a dash of Liquid Smoke adds depth.

Slow Cooker Size:
4 to 6 quart

Cook Time: 8 hours

Setting: Low

Serves 4

1 tablespoon olive oil
1 large yellow onion, chopped
1 celery rib, chopped
½ large green bell pepper, seeded and chopped
1 large garlic clove, minced
3 cups vegetable stock (see A Note About Stock, page 32)
2 cups tomato or vegetable juice
One 14.5-ounce can diced tomatoes, drained
2 medium-size zucchini, cut in half lengthwise and sliced into ¼-inch-thick half moons
1 teaspoon filé powder (optional)
1 teaspoon dried thyme
Salt and freshly ground black pepper
1 teaspoon Tabasco sauce, or to taste
½ teaspoon Liquid Smoke (optional)
2 cups hot cooked long-grain rice

1. Heat the oil in a large saucepan over medium heat. Add the onion, celery, bell pepper, and garlic, cover, and cook until softened, about 5 minutes.

2. Transfer the vegetables to a 4- to 6-quart slow cooker, add the stock, tomato juice, tomatoes, zucchini, filé powder, if using, and thyme, and season with salt and pepper. Cover and cook on Low for 8 hours.

3. Just before serving, stir in the Tabasco and Liquid Smoke, if using. Taste to adjust the seasonings. To serve, divide the cooked rice evenly into four soup bowls and top with the gumbo. Serve hot.

Old-Fashioned Vegetable Soup

This soup is as basic as it gets. Vary the vegetables according to personal preference and what's on hand and in season. For a more substantial soup, add some cooked pasta, rice, or other grain when ready to serve. For added flavor, sauté the onions, carrots, and celery in olive oil in a skillet for 5 to 10 minutes before adding to the cooker.

Slow Cooker Size:
6 quart

Cook Time: 8 hours

Setting: Low

Serves 4 to 6

1 tablespoon olive oil

2 medium-size carrots, chopped

1 medium-size yellow onion, chopped

1 celery rib, chopped

2 small red potatoes, left unpeeled and diced

½ small red bell pepper, seeded and chopped

4 ounces green beans, ends trimmed and cut into 1-inch pieces

1 large garlic clove, minced

6 cups vegetable stock (see A Note About Stock, page 32)

1½ cups slow-cooked (page 95) or one 15.5-ounce can navy or other small white beans, drained and rinsed

½ cup fresh or frozen green peas

Salt and freshly ground black pepper

2 tablespoons chopped fresh parsley leaves

1. Place the oil, carrots, onion, and celery in a 6-quart slow cooker, cover, and cook on High to soften slightly while you assemble the remaining ingredients.

2. Once prepped, add the potatoes, bell pepper, green beans, garlic, and stock to the cooker; cover, and cook on Low for 8 hours.

3. About 30 minutes before you're ready to serve, add the beans and peas and season with salt and pepper. Just before serving, stir in the parsley and taste to adjust the seasonings. Serve hot.

All-Day Minestrone

To save on cleanup time, the harder vegetables are softened directly in the slow cooker while you prepare the other ingredients. The soup's flavor is enriched by the addition of pesto sauce at the end of cooking time. If you are unable to add the raw pasta to the soup during the last hour of cooking, cook the pasta in advance, drain, rinse, and refrigerate. Then, when ready to serve, the cooked pasta can be combined with the soup at the last minute—it will heat quickly in the hot soup. I like to cook this soup in a 6-quart slow cooker to allow for the large amount of ingredients. A small cooker may be used, although you may need to cut back slightly on the amounts of everything to prevent overfilling.

Slow Cooker Size:
4 to 6 quart

Cook Time: 7 to 8 hours
(pasta added during
last hour of cooking)

Setting: Low

Serves 6

1 tablespoon olive oil
1 medium-size yellow onion, minced
1 celery rib, chopped
1 large carrot, chopped
2 garlic cloves, minced
4 ounces green beans, ends trimmed and cut into 1-inch pieces
1½ cups slow-cooked (page 95) or one 15.5-ounce can chickpeas, drained
  and rinsed
One 14.5-ounce can diced tomatoes, left undrained
1 medium-size zucchini or yellow summer squash, diced
6 cups vegetable stock (see A Note About Stock, page 32)
Salt and freshly ground black pepper
½ cup raw or 1 cup cooked *ditalini* or other small soup pasta
¼ cup pesto, homemade (page 51) or store-bought

1. Pour the oil in the bottom of a 4- to 6-quart slow cooker. Add the onion, celery, carrot, and garlic, cover, and cook on High while you assemble the remaining ingredients.

2. After they've been prepped, add the green beans, chickpeas, tomatoes, zucchini, and stock to the slow cooker and season with salt and pepper. Cover and cook on Low for 7 to 8 hours.

3. If using raw *ditalini*, about an hour before you're ready to serve, add it to the slow cooker and cover.

4. Just before serving, stir in the pesto and already-cooked pasta, if using.

Carrot and Parsnip Bisque with a Hint of Orange

Root vegetables team up to make this velvety bisque, its natural sweetness and lovely color enhanced by the addition of orange juice.

Slow Cooker Size:
4 to 6 quart

Cook Time: 8 hours

Setting: Low

Serves 6

1 tablespoon olive oil
1 medium-size yellow onion, chopped
3 large carrots, sliced
2 large parsnips, peeled and sliced
1 medium-size all-purpose potato, peeled and diced
1 garlic clove, minced
5 cups vegetable stock (see A Note About Stock, page 32)
Salt
Cayenne pepper
2 tablespoons frozen orange juice concentrate
2 tablespoons snipped fresh chives

1. Heat the oil in a large skillet over medium heat. Add the onion, carrots, parsnips, potato, and garlic; cover, and cook until softened, about 10 minutes.

2. Transfer the vegetables to a 4- to 6-quart slow cooker. Add the stock, season with salt and cayenne, cover, and cook on Low for 8 hours.

3. Working in batches, process the mixture in a blender or food processor until smooth, or use an immersion blender to purée the soup right in the slow cooker.

4. Just before serving, add the orange juice concentrate, stirring until it is melted. Taste the soup to adjust the seasonings. Serve garnished with a sprinkling of the chives.

Curried Cauliflower Soup with Chutney and Cashews

Cauliflower is frequently used in Indian curry dishes, and with good reason—the flavors complement each other beautifully. The addition of chutney provides a note of sweetness and amplifies the flavor of the curry, while the cashews add a bit of crunch.

Slow Cooker Size:
6 quart

Cook Time: 6 hours

Setting: Low

Serves 6

1 tablespoon peanut or other mild-tasting oil
1 medium-size yellow onion, chopped
1 small carrot, chopped
2 teaspoons curry powder or paste
1 medium-size head cauliflower, trimmed and chopped
1 medium-size Yukon Gold potato, peeled and diced
6 cups vegetable stock (see A Note About Stock, page 32)
Salt
¼ cup mango chutney
¼ cup chopped roasted cashews
1 tablespoon minced fresh parsley leaves

1. Heat the oil in a medium-size skillet over medium heat. Add the onion and carrot, cover, and cook until softened, about 5 minutes. Add the curry powder and stir to coat the vegetables.

2. Transfer the onion mixture to a 6-quart slow cooker. Add the cauliflower, potato, and stock; season with salt, cover, and cook on Low for 6 hours.

3. Add the chutney and, working in batches, purée the soup in a blender or food processor, or use an immersion blender to purée the soup right in the cooker. Taste and adjust the seasonings if necessary. Serve garnished with a sprinkling of the cashews and parsley.

Corn Chowder in Winter

When you crave fresh corn in the middle of winter, this chowder can help. Made with frozen corn kernels, you get the sweet, creamy taste of corn in every spoonful. Of course, the chowder can also be made with fresh corn when it is available with delicious results (you would need the kernels from 6 ears). No milk or cream is used in this recipe—the chowder gets its thickness by puréeing some of the vegetables in the soup. Put a bottle of Tabasco on the table for those who like heat.

Slow Cooker Size:
4 to 6 quart

Cook Time: 6 hours

Setting: Low

Serves 4

1 tablespoon olive oil
1 small yellow onion, chopped
1 celery rib, chopped
1 large Yukon Gold potato, peeled and diced
3 cups frozen corn kernels
½ small yellow bell pepper, seeded and chopped
4 cups vegetable stock (see A Note About Stock, page 32)
Salt and freshly ground black pepper
1 large ripe tomato, seeded and chopped
1 tablespoon snipped fresh chives, parsley, or other fresh herbs
   (try Thai basil for an interesting flavor accent)

1. Heat the oil in a large skillet over medium heat. Add onion and celery, cover, and cook until softened, about 5 minutes.

2. Transfer the cooked vegetables to a 4- to 6-quart slow cooker. Add the potato, corn, bell pepper, and stock; season with salt and pepper, cover, and cook on Low for 6 hours.

3. Ladle 2 cups of the soup solids into a food processor or blender and process until smooth. Stir the purée back into the chowder and taste for salt and pepper. To serve, ladle the soup into bowls and garnish with the chopped tomato and chives or other fresh herbs.

Winter Squash and Sweet Potato Soup

This soup is a great way to begin Thanksgiving dinner. Best of all, when made in a slow cooker, it frees up the already-crowded stovetop and keeps the soup at a good serving temperature while everyone gathers at the table.

Slow Cooker Size:
4 to 6 quart

Cook Time: 6 hours

Setting: Low

Serves 4 to 6

1 tablespoon olive oil
1 small yellow onion, chopped
1 celery rib, chopped
2 medium-size sweet potatoes, peeled and diced
1 small butternut squash, peeled, seeded, and thinly sliced
4 cups vegetable stock (see A Note About Stock, page 32)
1 teaspoon dried thyme
½ teaspoon dried sage
Salt and freshly ground black pepper

1. Heat the oil in a large skillet over medium heat. Add the onion and celery, cover, and cook until softened, about 5 minutes.

2. Transfer the cooked vegetables to a 4- to 6-quart slow cooker. Add the sweet potatoes, squash, stock, thyme, and sage; season with salt and pepper, cover, and cook on Low for 6 hours.

3. Purée the soup in a blender or food processor, working in batches, or directly in the slow cooker using an immersion blender. Taste to adjust the seasonings, and serve hot.

Chipotle-Potato Soup with Frizzled Leeks

The smoky heat of the chipotle chiles is mellowed by the mild creaminess of Yukon Gold potatoes. The chipotles are swirled in at the end because it produces a lovely color effect and it also allows you to add as much or as little to each serving as desired. The leek garnish adds an unexpected textural element. Chipotle chiles in adobo sauce are available in most supermarkets and specialty grocers.

Slow Cooker Size:
4 quart

Cook Time: 6 to 8 hours

Setting: Low

Serves 6

2 leeks (white part only), trimmed and well washed
2 tablespoons olive oil
1½ pounds Yukon Gold potatoes, peeled and diced
6 cups vegetable stock (see A Note About Stock, page 32)
Salt
1 or 2 canned chipotle chiles in adobo sauce, to taste

1. Coarsely chop one of the leeks and set the other one aside.

2. Place 1 tablespoon of the oil in a 4-quart slow cooker. Add the chopped leek, cover, and cook on High to soften while you prepare the remaining ingredients.

3. Once they're prepped, add the potatoes and stock to the cooker; season with salt, cover, and cook on Low for 6 to 8 hours.

4. While the soup is cooking, finely cut the remaining leek into very thin matchsticks. Heat the remaining 1 tablespoon oil in a small skillet over medium-high heat. Add the leek and cook, stirring frequently, until the pieces are browned and "frizzled," then transfer to a paper towel to drain. Set aside until ready to serve the soup.

5. Process the chiles in a blender or food processor until smooth and set aside.

6. When the potatoes are soft, use an immersion blender to purée the soup right in the slow cooker. Otherwise, purée the soup in batches in a blender or food processor, returning it to the cooker to keep warm. Taste to adjust the seasonings.

7. To serve, ladle the soup into bowls, swirl a small amount of the chipotle purée into each serving according to taste, and top with a sprinkling of the leeks.

Pesto-Potato Soup with Toasted Pine Nuts

Pesto turns humble potato soup into a bold flavor statement punctuated by the crunch of toasted pine nuts. The pesto will keep, refrigerated, for several weeks when topped with a thin layer of olive oil and stored in a tightly sealed container.

Slow Cooker Size:
4 to 6 quart

Cook Time: 6 to 8 hours

Setting: Low

Serves 6

Soup

2 tablespoons olive oil

3 garlic cloves, minced

1½ pounds Yukon Gold potatoes, peeled and diced

6 cups vegetable stock (see A Note About Stock, page 32)

Salt

Pesto

2 large garlic cloves, peeled

¼ cup pine nuts

2 cups firmly packed fresh basil leaves

½ teaspoon salt

Freshly ground black pepper

⅓ cup extra-virgin olive oil

Garnish

¼ cup pine nuts, toasted (page 16)

1. To make the soup, place the oil and garlic in a 4- to 6-quart slow cooker, cover, and cook on High while you prep the potatoes or long enough to slightly soften the garlic and bring out its flavor. Once prepped, add the potatoes and stock and season with salt. Cover and cook on Low for 6 to 8 hours.

2. To make the pesto, combine the garlic and pine nuts in a food processor or blender and pulse until coarsely chopped. Add the basil, salt, and pepper to taste and process until ground into a paste. With the machine running, stream in the olive oil through the feed tube, processing until well blended. Set aside until ready to serve the soup.

3. When the potatoes are soft, use an immersion blender to purée the soup right in the slow cooker. Otherwise, purée the soup in batches in a blender or food processor, returning it to the cooker to keep warm. Taste to adjust the seasonings.

4. To serve, ladle the soup into bowls, swirl a spoonful of pesto into each serving and garnish with a sprinkling of toasted pine nuts.

French Onion Soup with Cheesy Bruschetta

As anyone fond of French onion soup can attest, the best onion soup is one that is simmered long and slow to coax the most flavor out of the onions. What better way to accomplish this than with a slow cooker? The cheesy bruschetta topping offers an easy alternative to placing unwieldy soup crocks under the broiler.

Slow Cooker Size:
4 to 6 quart

Cook Time:
8½ to 11 hours

Setting: 8 to 10 hours on Low; 30 to 60 minutes on High

Serves 6

¼ cup olive oil
4 medium-size Vidalia or other sweet onions, thinly sliced
5½ cups vegetable stock (see A Note About Stock, page 32)
⅓ cup brandy (optional)
Salt and freshly ground black pepper
Cheesy Bruschetta (recipe follows)

1. Spread the oil in the bottom of a 4- to 6-quart slow cooker, add the onions, cover, and cook on Low for 8 to 10 hours or longer, until the onions are very soft and well caramelized.

2. Add the stock and brandy, if using, and season with salt and pepper. Cover and cook on High for 30 minutes to an hour, until hot.

3. While the soup is heating, make the bruschetta (recipe follows).

4. To serve, ladle the soup into bowls and float a bruschetta on top of each serving or serve alongside. Serve immediately.

Cheesy Bruschetta

6 slices French or Italian bread, ½ inch thick
6 slices Fontina cheese or soy mozzarella

Preheat the broiler. Place the bread slices on a baking sheet, top with the cheese, and run them under the broiler until the cheese is melted, being careful not to burn them. Serve immediately.

Serves 6

"Seeing Red" Borscht

It took me all the way to adulthood to appreciate the flavor of beets. Now, I can't seem to get enough of them, whether roasted, tossed in salads, or featured in this lovely scarlet soup that can be eaten hot or cold. The optional barley miso adds depth of flavor and lots of nutrients, but because it is salty, you'll need to watch how much salt you add.

Slow Cooker Size:
4 to 6 quart

Cook Time: 8 hours

Setting: Low

Serves 6

2 pounds beets, peeled and chopped
1 large yellow onion, finely chopped
1 small carrot, finely chopped
1 small red bell pepper, seeded and finely chopped
1 large all-purpose potato, peeled and diced
5 cups vegetable stock (see A Note About Stock, page 32)
1 tablespoon fresh lemon juice
2 teaspoons light brown sugar or a natural sweetener
1 teaspoon dried thyme
½ teaspoon ground cloves
Salt and freshly ground black pepper
1 tablespoon barley miso dissolved in 1 tablespoon hot water (optional)
Regular or soy sour cream (optional garnish)
2 tablespoons minced fresh dill or 1½ teaspoons dillweed

1. In a 4- to 6-quart slow cooker, combine the beets, onion, carrot, bell pepper, and potato. Add the stock, lemon juice, sugar, thyme, and cloves and season with salt and pepper. Cover and cook on Low for 8 hours.

2. Just before serving, stir in the miso mixture, if using. Serve hot or allow to cool and refrigerate until well chilled. Garnish with the sour cream, if using, and the dill.

Note: To save prep time, you may shred all the vegetables in a food processor using the shredding disc. This will change the texture of the soup, but some people prefer it this way.

Tortilla Tomato Soup

Crispy tortilla strips add texture to this creamy tomato soup, while the optional tequila adds a lively kick. With or without the tequila, this is definitely not the canned tomato soup you ate as a child.

Slow Cooker Size:
4 quart

Cook Time: 6 to 8 hours

Setting: Low

Serves 4

1 tablespoon olive oil
1 medium-size yellow onion, chopped
1 celery rib, minced
One 28-ounce can crushed tomatoes
¼ cup tomato paste
3 cups vegetable stock (see A Note About Stock, page 32)
Salt and freshly ground black pepper
2 soft corn tortillas
1 tablespoon fresh lime juice
1 tablespoon chopped fresh parsley leaves
1 teaspoon chopped fresh cilantro leaves
1 teaspoon ground cumin
¼ cup tequila (optional)
Diced avocado for garnish (optional)
Sliced black olives for garnish (optional)

1. Heat the oil in a large saucepan over medium heat. Add the onion and celery, cover, and cook until softened, about 5 minutes.

2. Transfer the cooked vegetables to a 4-quart slow cooker, add the tomatoes, tomato paste, and stock, and season with salt and pepper. Cover and cook on Low for 6 to 8 hours.

3. While the soup is cooking, prepare the tortillas: Place the tortillas in a lightly oiled skillet and cook until crisp on both sides. Cut into strips and set aside.

4. Shortly before serving time, stir in the lime juice, parsley, cilantro, cumin, and tequila, if using. Working in batches if necessary, purée the soup in a blender or food processor or purée directly in the slow cooker using an immersion blender. Taste to adjust the seasonings. Ladle into bowls and top with the tortilla strips and avocado and olives, if using. Serve hot.

Creamy Tomato Soup with Israeli Couscous

Israeli couscous is distinctly different from regular couscous in appearance and flavor. About the size of peppercorns, Israeli couscous can be found in well-stocked supermarkets and gourmet grocers. If unavailable, substitute *acini di pepe* (peppercorn) pasta, or another small soup pasta such as orzo or *ditalini*.

Slow Cooker Size:
4 quart

Cook Time: 6 to 8 hours

Setting: Low

Serves 4

1 tablespoon olive oil
1 medium-size yellow onion, chopped
1 garlic clove, minced
3 cups vegetable stock (see A Note About Stock, page 32)
One 28-ounce can crushed tomatoes
1 tablespoon tomato paste
Pinch of sugar or a natural sweetener
2 bay leaves
Salt and freshly ground black pepper
1 cup cooked Israeli couscous
2 tablespoons chopped fresh basil leaves for garnish

1. Heat the oil in a medium-size skillet over medium heat. Add the onion and garlic, cover, and cook until softened, about 5 minutes.

2. Transfer the vegetables to a 4-quart slow cooker, add the stock, tomatoes, tomato paste, sugar, and bay leaves, and season with salt and pepper. Cover and cook on Low for 6 to 8 hours. Purée the soup in a food processor or blender or use an immersion blender to purée it in the slow cooker. Adjust the seasonings and remove the bay leaves.

3. To serve, spoon about ¼ cup of cooked couscous into the bottom of each bowl, ladle the hot soup on top, and serve sprinkled with the basil.

Two-Mushroom Barley Soup

Both dried and fresh mushrooms are used in this satisfying soup popular throughout Eastern Europe. Any kind of dried mushroom is fine for this soup—I especially like the woodsy flavor of porcini. Pearl barley can be found in most supermarkets or health food stores.

Slow Cooker Size:
4 to 6 quart

Cook Time: 6 hours

Setting: Low

Serves 4 to 6

1 ounce dried mushrooms
1 tablespoon olive oil
1 medium-size yellow onion, chopped
1 large carrot, chopped
1 celery rib, chopped
1 cup pearl barley
8 ounces white mushrooms, sliced
6 cups vegetable stock (see A Note About Stock, page 32)
1½ teaspoons dried thyme
Salt and freshly ground black pepper
2 tablespoons minced fresh chives

1. Place the dried mushrooms in a heatproof measuring cup and cover with hot water. Let sit until softened. Drain, straining and reserving ½ cup of the soaking liquid, thinly slice the mushrooms, and set aside.

2. Heat the oil in a small skillet over medium heat. Add the onion, carrot, and celery, cover, and cook until softened, about 5 minutes.

3. Transfer the cooked vegetables to a 4- to 6-quart slow cooker. Add the barley, both kinds of mushrooms, the stock, the reserved mushroom liquid, and thyme and season with salt and pepper. Cover and cook on Low for 6 hours. Taste to adjust the seasonings before serving. If a thinner soup is desired, add more stock.

4. Serve garnished with the chives.

Slow Pho

Slow-cooking is a great way to develop the deep, rich flavor of *pho*, the Vietnamese noodle soup. Traditionally made with beef, this version is made with seitan or "wheat-meat." Rice sticks, miso paste, seitan, and hoisin sauce are all available in well-stocked supermarkets, natural food stores, and Asian markets. Look for star anise in super-markets and Asian markets. If unavailable, you can leave it out without seriously altering the flavor of the soup.

Slow Cooker Size:
4 quart

Cook Time: 6 hours

Setting: Low

Serves 4

1 small yellow onion, coarsely chopped

1 small green chile, seeded and chopped

3 slices fresh ginger

2 whole star anise

1 cinnamon stick

3 tablespoons tamari or other soy sauce

5 cups vegetable stock (see A Note About Stock, page 32)

1 tablespoon peanut oil

4 ounces seitan, cut into strips

3 tablespoons hoisin sauce

1½ tablespoons fresh lime juice

2 tablespoons barley miso paste dissolved in 2 tablespoons hot water

6 ounces dried rice sticks, soaked 15 minutes in cold water to soften, then drained

½ cup fresh bean sprouts for garnish

4 scallions, chopped, for garnish

2 tablespoons chopped fresh cilantro leaves for garnish

1. In a 4-quart slow cooker, combine the onion, chile, ginger, anise, cinnamon stick, tamari, and stock; cover, and cook on Low for 6 hours.

2. Meanwhile or beforehand, heat the oil in a large skillet over medium-high heat, add the seitan strips, and brown on all sides. Remove from the heat and set aside.

3. Strain the stock and return the broth to the cooker.

4. In a small bowl, combine the hoisin, lime juice, and miso paste mixture, then add to the broth. Stir in the drained rice sticks and seitan and cook 5 to 10 minutes longer, or until the rice sticks are soft.

5. To serve, ladle the soup into bowls and garnish with the bean sprouts, scallions, and cilantro.

Hot and Sour Soup

The slow cooker is a good way to coax the flavor of ginger, mushrooms, and other ingredients into the broth. If you prefer a less spicy version, cut back or eliminate the chile paste. Diced firm tofu may be substituted for the seitan, but it should be added near the end of the cooking time.

Slow Cooker Size:
4 quart

Cook Time: 6 to 8 hours

Setting: Low

Serves 4

⅓ cup dried shiitake or cloud ear mushrooms
4 ounces seitan, cut into thin slivers
One 6-ounce can bamboo shoots, drained, rinsed, and cut into thin strips
2 garlic cloves, minced
1 tablespoon peeled and minced fresh ginger
4 cups vegetable stock (see A Note About Stock, page 32)
2 tablespoons rice vinegar
2 tablespoons tamari or other soy sauce
1 teaspoon Asian chile paste
Salt and freshly ground black pepper
½ cup frozen peas, thawed
3 tablespoons minced scallions
1 tablespoon toasted sesame oil

1. Soak the dried mushrooms in a bowl of hot water for 20 minutes to soften. Drain, cut into thin strips, and place in a 4-quart slow cooker. Add the seitan, bamboo shoots, garlic, ginger, stock, vinegar, tamari, and chile paste. Season with salt and pepper, cover, and cook on Low for 6 to 8 hours.

2. Just before serving, stir in the peas, scallions, and sesame oil. Serve hot.

Chinese Hot Pot

Hot in temperature and flavor, this vegetarian version of the classic Chinese soup is fragrant and delicious. I like to add some cooked rice at serving time for a substantial one-dish meal.

Slow Cooker Size:
4 quart

Cook Time: 8 hours

Setting: Low

Serves 4

1 small yellow onion, chopped
1 large carrot, halved lengthwise and thinly sliced on a diagonal
1 celery rib, thinly sliced on a diagonal
One 6-ounce can sliced water chestnuts, drained
2 garlic cloves, finely minced
1 teaspoon peeled and grated fresh ginger
¼ teaspoon red pepper flakes, or to taste
5½ cups vegetable stock (see A Note About Stock, page 32)
1 tablespoon tamari or other soy sauce
8 ounces extra-firm tofu, drained and diced
4 ounces fresh shiitake mushrooms, stemmed and caps thinly sliced
1 ounce snow peas, strings trimmed and cut into 1-inch pieces
3 scallions, chopped
½ teaspoon toasted sesame oil or Chinese hot oil

1. In a 4-quart slow cooker, combine the onion, carrot, celery, water chestnuts, garlic, ginger, and red pepper flakes. Add the stock and tamari, cover, and cook on Low for 8 hours.

2. About 20 minutes before serving, add the tofu, mushrooms, snow peas, and scallions. Drizzle on the sesame oil, cover, and cook until the mushrooms and snow peas are tender. Serve immediately.

Chilis and Stews

. . .

Like soups, stews and chilis are ideal candi-
dates for the slow cooker. The extra-rich flavor that comes
from slow cooking is especially noticeable in a stew, where
a variety of ingredients have the opportunity to mingle.
When it's ready, you have a complete one-dish meal with no
messy cleanup—cook and serve everything in one pot.

Virtually all the recipes in this chapter begin by cooking the onions
and other chopped vegetables in a skillet for a few minutes to soften
them. If you're tempted to omit this step, I would strongly urge you not
to. Cooking the veggies first will not only give your stew or chili more
flavor, but will aid in the cooking process so that the vegetables will be
tender enough to eat when you're ready. Cooking the onions and other
hard vegetables on the higher temperature of the stovetop will bring out
more of their flavor and soften them relatively quickly. However, if you
prefer not to dirty the extra pan (and you have the extra time), I suggest
that you at least cook them in the slow cooker on High to soften them.
Since this can take a while (about 15 minutes for minced garlic, about 30
minutes for chopped onion), you will need to weigh whether or not the
extra time is worth having one less pot to wash. To skip the step alto-
gether can mean hard veggies, especially in stews and chilis where there's
not as much liquid to help them soften as in soups.

Sweet and Spicy Lentil Chili

Molasses and apple juice add sweetness to this dare-to-be-different chili made with lentils. Slow cooking helps to round out the flavors, culminating in delicious harmony.

Slow Cooker Size:
4 quart

Cook Time: 8 hours

Setting: Low

Serves 4 to 6

1 tablespoon olive oil
1 large sweet yellow onion, chopped
1 small red bell pepper, seeded and chopped
2 garlic cloves, minced
2 tablespoons chili powder, or to taste
1½ cups dried brown lentils, picked over and rinsed
One 28-ounce can crushed tomatoes
⅓ cup dark unsulfured molasses
½ teaspoon ground allspice
Cayenne pepper to taste
Salt and freshly ground black pepper
2 cups water
1 cup apple juice

1. Heat the oil in a large skillet over medium heat. Add the onion, bell pepper, and garlic, cover, and cook until softened, about 5 minutes. Stir in the chili powder and cook about 30 seconds longer.

2. Transfer the mixture to a 4-quart slow cooker. Add the lentils, tomatoes, molasses, and allspice and season with cayenne, salt, and black pepper. Stir in the water and apple juice, cover, and cook on Low for 8 hours. Add more water if the chili gets too thick.

Farm Stand Chili with Chickpeas

Loads of vegetables are what make this chili stand out from the crowd. It's a good choice in the summer when you crave the flavor of chili but want to take advantage of the season's produce. And slow cooking won't heat up the kitchen.

Slow Cooker Size:
4 to 6 quart

Cook Time: 6 to 8 hours

Setting: Low

Serves 6

1 tablespoon olive oil
1 large sweet yellow onion, chopped
1 celery rib, minced
1 medium-size eggplant, peeled and chopped
1 small red bell pepper, seeded and chopped
1 garlic clove, finely minced
1 tablespoon chili powder, or more to taste
1 small red or green chile (optional), seeded and finely minced
1½ cups water
One 14.5-ounce can diced tomatoes, with their juices
1½ cups slow-cooked (page 95) or one 15.5-ounce can chickpeas, drained and rinsed
1 cup fresh or thawed frozen corn kernels
Salt and freshly ground black pepper

1. Heat the oil in a large skillet over medium heat. Add the onion, celery, eggplant, bell pepper, and garlic, cover, and cook until softened, about 5 minutes. Stir in the chili powder and chile, if using, and cook 30 seconds longer.

2. Transfer the vegetables to a 4- to 6-quart slow cooker and add the water, tomatoes, chickpeas, and corn, and season with salt and pepper. Cover and cook on Low for 6 to 8 hours.

Spicy Black Bean Chili

This dark, rich chili is so easy to make, and it's full of flavor, thanks to its long, slow cooking. For dramatic accompaniments, serve over noodles or rice made golden with a pinch of turmeric, and top with some diced avocado.

Slow Cooker Size:
4 to 6 quart

Cook time: 6 to 8 hours

Setting: Low

Serves 4

1 tablespoon olive oil
1 large yellow onion, chopped
1 medium-size red bell pepper, seeded and chopped
2 garlic cloves, minced
2 tablespoons chili powder, or more to taste
One 28-ounce can crushed tomatoes
3 cups slow-cooked (page 95) or two 15.5-ounce cans black beans, drained and rinsed
1 cup water
One 4-ounce can diced green chiles, drained
Salt and freshly ground black pepper

1. Heat the oil in a large skillet over medium heat. Add the onion, bell pepper, and garlic; cover, and cook until just softened, about 5 minutes. Stir in the chili powder and cook about 30 seconds longer.

2. Transfer the mixture to a 4- to 6-quart slow cooker. Add the tomatoes, beans, water, and chiles; season with salt and pepper, cover, and cook on Low for 6 to 8 hours.

Three-Bean Chili with Chive-Flecked Cornmeal Dumplings

Cornmeal dumplings add down-home goodness to this hearty chili made with three different kinds of beans.

Slow Cooker Size:
4 to 6 quart

Cook Time: 6 to 8 hours for chili; 30 to 40 minutes for dumplings

Setting: Low for chili; High for dumplings

Serves 4 to 6

Chili

1 tablespoon olive oil

1 large sweet yellow onion, chopped

½ small green bell pepper, seeded and chopped

2 garlic cloves, minced

3 tablespoons tomato paste

1 tablespoon chili powder, or more to taste

One 28-ounce can crushed tomatoes

1½ cups slow-cooked (page 95) or one 15.5-ounce can black beans, drained and rinsed

1½ cups slow-cooked (page 95) or one 15.5-ounce can pinto beans, drained and rinsed

1½ cups slow-cooked (page 95) or one 15.5-ounce can kidney beans, drained and rinsed

1½ cups water

1 teaspoon salt

¼ teaspoon freshly ground black pepper

Dumplings

⅔ cup all-purpose flour

⅓ cup yellow cornmeal

2 teaspoons baking powder

1 teaspoon minced fresh chives

⅛ teaspoon salt

½ cup fresh or thawed frozen corn kernels

½ cup milk or soy milk

2 tablespoons olive oil

1. To make the chili, heat the oil in a large skillet over medium heat. Add the onion, bell pepper, and garlic, cover, and cook until softened, about 5 minutes. Stir in the tomato paste and chili powder and cook about 30 seconds longer.

2. Transfer the mixture to a 4- to 6-quart slow cooker. Add the tomatoes, beans, and water, season with salt and pepper, cover, and cook on Low for 6 to 8 hours.

3. To make the dumplings, combine the flour, cornmeal, baking powder, chives, and salt in a medium-size bowl about 45 minutes before serving time. Stir in the corn, milk, and oil until just combined. Do not overmix.

4. Turn the slow cooker to High and drop the batter by the spoonful onto the hot chili. Cover and cook on High until the dumplings are cooked through, 30 to 40 minutes. Serve immediately.

Chipotle-Kissed Red Bean and Sweet Potato Chili

The vibrant red and orange colors make this chili appealing to the eye as well as the taste buds. If the smoky heat of the chipotle chile is not to your liking, try this recipe without it for a full-flavored, yet mild, chili.

Slow Cooker Size:
4 to 6 quart

Cook Time: 6 to 8 hours

Setting: Low

Serves 4 to 6

1 tablespoon olive oil
1 medium-size yellow onion, chopped
1 medium-size red bell pepper, seeded and chopped
1 large garlic clove, minced
1 tablespoon chili powder, or more to taste
1½ pounds sweet potatoes, peeled and cut into ½-inch chunks
One 14.5-ounce can crushed tomatoes
1½ cups slow-cooked (page 95) or one 15.5-ounce can dark red
    kidney beans, drained and rinsed
1½ cups water
Salt
1 tablespoon minced canned chipotle chiles in adobo sauce, or to taste

1. Heat the oil in a large skillet over medium heat. Add the onion, bell pepper, and garlic, cover, and cook until softened, about 5 minutes. Stir in the chili powder and cook for 30 seconds. Add the sweet potatoes and stir to coat with the spices.

2. Transfer the mixture to a 4- to 6-quart slow cooker. Add the tomatoes, beans, and water; season with salt, cover, and cook on Low for 6 to 8 hours.

3. When ready to serve, stir the chipotles into the chili. Taste to adjust the seasonings.

Perfect Hominy White Bean Chili

Hominy—dried corn kernels from which the germ and the hull have been removed—has a natural affinity for chili spices. Canned hominy has been reconstituted and is ready to eat. For a less spicy chili, omit the jalapeño.

Slow Cooker Size:
4 to 6 quart

Cook Time: 6 to 8 hours

Setting: Low

Serves 4 to 6

1 tablespoon olive oil

1 small yellow onion, diced

2 garlic cloves, minced

1 tablespoon chili powder, or more to taste

1 jalapeño chile (optional), seeded and chopped

One 14.5-ounce can crushed tomatoes

3 cups slow-cooked (page 95) or two 15.5-ounce cans navy or other white beans, drained and rinsed

One 16-ounce can hominy, drained and rinsed

1½ cups water

½ teaspoon ground cumin

½ teaspoon dried oregano

1 teaspoon salt

¼ teaspoon freshly ground black pepper

2 tablespoons chopped fresh cilantro leaves

1. Heat the oil in a large skillet over medium heat. Add the onion and garlic, cover, and cook until softened, about 5 minutes. Stir in the chili powder and cook about 30 seconds longer.

2. Transfer the mixture to a 4- to 6-quart slow cooker. Add the jalapeño, tomatoes, beans, hominy, water, cumin, oregano, salt, and pepper; cover, and cook on Low for 6 to 8 hours.

3. Just before serving, stir in the cilantro and taste to adjust the seasonings.

Spicy White Bean and Sweet Potato Stew with Collards

This stew is colorful and full flavored, thanks to a host of vegetables and seasonings. I like to cook the collard greens separately to avoid any bitter taste in the stew. Because sweet potatoes break down easily, it's important not to cook this stew too long. For a mild, yet still flavorful, version, eliminate the hot chile. Serve it accompanied by crusty warm bread.

Slow Cooker Size:
4 to 6 quart

Cook Time: 4 to 6 hours

Setting: Low

Serves 4 to 6

1 tablespoon olive oil

1 medium-size yellow onion, chopped

1 small red bell pepper, seeded and chopped

2 garlic cloves, minced

1 pound sweet potatoes, peeled and cut into 1-inch chunks

1 fresh hot chile, seeded and minced

1 teaspoon peeled and grated fresh ginger

One 14.5-ounce can diced tomatoes, with their juices

3 cups slow-cooked (page 95) or two 15.5-ounce cans cannellini beans, drained and rinsed

1 teaspoon light brown sugar or a natural sweetener

½ teaspoon ground allspice

¼ teaspoon ground cumin

2 bay leaves

3 cups vegetable stock (see A Note About Stock, page 32)

Salt and freshly ground black pepper

2 cups chopped collard greens, cooked in simmering water until tender and drained

1. Heat the oil in a large skillet over medium heat. Add the onion, bell pepper, and garlic. Cover, and cook until softened, about 5 minutes.

2. Transfer the mixture to a 4- to 6-quart slow cooker. Add the sweet potatoes, chile, ginger, tomatoes, beans, brown sugar, allspice, cumin, bay leaves, and stock; season with salt and pepper, cover, and cook on Low for 4 to 6 hours.

3. Close to serving time, stir in the cooked collard greens. Taste to adjust the seasonings, remove the bay leaves, and serve.

Pesto-Infused White Bean and Sun-Dried Tomato Stew

The flavors of Italy combine in this stew that is especially good served over pasta or with grilled Italian bread. If fresh ripe tomatoes are unavailable, use canned tomatoes instead.

Slow Cooker Size:
4 quart

Cook Time: 6 to 8 hours

Setting: Low

Serves 4

1 tablespoon olive oil
1 large Vidalia or other sweet onion, chopped
1 red bell pepper, seeded and cut into ¼-inch dice
3 large ripe tomatoes, peeled, seeded, and chopped
¼ cup chopped sun-dried tomatoes
3 cups slow-cooked (page 95) or two 15.5-ounce cans cannellini or
    other white beans, drained and rinsed
1½ cups vegetable stock (see A Note About Stock, page 32)
Salt and freshly ground black pepper
¼ cup pesto, homemade (page 51) or store-bought

1. Heat the oil in a medium-size skillet over medium heat. Add the onion, cover, and cook until softened, about 5 minutes.

2. Transfer the onion to a 4-quart slow cooker. Add the bell pepper, both kinds of tomatoes, the beans, and stock; season with salt and pepper, cover, and cook on Low for 6 to 8 hours.

3. Just before serving, stir in the pesto. Taste to adjust the seasonings.

Ready and Waiting Bean and Vegetable Ragout

This is the perfect stew for a chilly fall night when hectic schedules can put home-cooked meals in jeopardy. Turn the tables and have this hearty and wholesome stew ready and waiting when you get home. If your day stretches longer than eight hours, use an electric timer to start your cooker up to two hours after you leave the house.

Slow Cooker Size:
4 to 6 quart

Cook Time: 6 to 8 hours

Setting: Low

Serves 6

2 tablespoons olive oil

1 medium-size yellow onion, finely chopped

1 large carrot, halved lengthwise and sliced into half moons

1 large turnip, peeled and diced

1 large parsnip, peeled, halved lengthwise, and sliced into half moons

1 large sweet potato, peeled and diced

1½ cups slow-cooked (page 95) or one 15.5-ounce can cannellini or other white beans, drained and rinsed

2 cups vegetable stock (see A Note About Stock, page 32)

½ cup dry white wine

1 teaspoon minced fresh thyme leaves or ½ teaspoon dried

1 teaspoon salt

¼ teaspoon freshly ground black pepper

1 cup cooked chopped collards or other dark leafy greens

1. Heat the oil in a large skillet over medium heat. Add the onion and carrot, cover, and cook until softened, about 5 minutes.

2. Transfer the cooked vegetables to a 4- to 6-quart slow cooker. Add the turnip, parsnip, sweet potato, beans, stock, wine, thyme, salt, and pepper; cover, and cook on Low for 6 to 8 hours.

3. About 10 minutes before ready to serve, stir in the cooked collards. Serve hot.

Almost Irish Stew

With the slow cooker doing all the work, you will have time to make a loaf of soda bread to accompany this "almost Irish" stew. Chunks of seitan may be substituted for the beans for a "meatier" alternative.

Slow Cooker Size:
4 to 6 quart

Cook Time: 6 to 8 hours

Setting: Low

Serves 4

1 tablespoon olive oil
1 small yellow onion, chopped
1½ cups baby carrots, halved lengthwise
6 very small white potatoes, halved or quartered
2 garlic cloves, minced
1½ cups slow-cooked (page 95) or one 15.5-ounce can cannellini beans, drained and rinsed
2 cups vegetable stock (see A Note About Stock, page 32)
1 bay leaf
¼ cup dry white wine
2 tablespoons tamari or other soy sauce
1 teaspoon dried thyme
Salt and freshly ground black pepper
3 large kale leaves or other dark leafy greens, chopped, cooked in simmering water to cover until tender, and drained

1. Heat the oil in a large skillet over medium heat. Add the onion, cover, and cook until softened, about 5 minutes.

2. Transfer the onions to a 4- to 6-quart slow cooker. Add the carrots, potatoes, garlic, beans, stock, bay leaf, wine, tamari, and thyme and season with salt and pepper. Cover and cook on Low for 6 to 8 hours.

3. About 10 minutes before serving, stir in the cooked kale. Serve hot.

Red, White, and Blue Stew

It doesn't have to be the Fourth of July to serve up this patriotic stew, but it's not a bad idea then either, since the slow cooker won't heat up the kitchen even in the middle of summer. Blue potatoes are available in well-stocked supermarkets. If you can't find them, use red or white potatoes and serve with blue corn chips to carry the theme.

Slow Cooker Size:
4 to 6 quart

Cook Time: 6 to 8 hours

Setting: Low

Serves 4 to 6

1 tablespoon olive oil

1 large red onion, chopped

1 small red bell pepper, seeded and chopped

2 garlic cloves, minced

1 pound small blue potatoes, left unpeeled and halved or quartered, depending on size

1½ cups slow-cooked (page 95) or one 15.5-ounce can dark red kidney beans, drained and rinsed

1½ cups slow-cooked (page 95) or one 15.5-ounce can cannellini or other white beans, drained and rinsed

3 cups vegetable stock (see A Note About Stock, page 32)

¼ cup dry white wine

2 tablespoons tamari or other soy sauce

1 bay leaf

1 teaspoon dried thyme

Salt and freshly ground black pepper

1. Heat the oil in a large skillet over medium heat. Add the onion, bell pepper, and garlic; cover, and cook until just softened, about 5 minutes.

2. Transfer the cooked vegetables to a 4- to 6-quart slow cooker. Add the potatoes, beans, stock, wine, tamari, bay leaf, and thyme and season with salt and pepper. Cover and cook on Low for 6 to 8 hours.

Indian Cauliflower and Kidney Bean Stew with Coconut Milk

The cauliflower and potatoes readily absorb the flavors of the spices and other seasonings in this popular Indian mélange. Puréeing the onion and spices together before cooking helps to bring out their flavors in the stew. Warm *roti*, *paratha*, or other Indian flatbread makes a good accompaniment.

Slow Cooker Size:
4 to 6 quart

Cook Time: 6 hours

Setting: Low

Serves 4 to 6

1 large yellow onion, cut into pieces
2 garlic cloves, sliced
1 teaspoon peeled and minced fresh ginger
1 jalapeño chile (optional), seeded
2 tablespoons olive oil
½ teaspoon dry mustard
½ teaspoon ground fennel seeds
½ teaspoon ground cardamom
½ teaspoon ground allspice
¼ teaspoon ground cumin
¼ teaspoon turmeric
¼ teaspoon cayenne pepper
2 large Yukon Gold potatoes, peeled and diced
½ head cauliflower, cut into small florets
1½ cups slow-cooked (page 95) or one 15.5-ounce can dark red kidney beans, drained and rinsed
One 14.5-ounce can diced tomatoes, drained
2 cups vegetable stock (see A Note About Stock, page 32)
Salt and freshly ground black pepper
1 cup canned unsweetened coconut milk

1. In a food processor, place the onion, garlic, ginger, and jalapeño, if using, and process until smooth.

2. Place the oil in a 4- to 6-quart slow cooker turned on High. Add the onion purée and stir in the mustard, fennel, cardamom, allspice, cumin, turmeric, and cayenne. Cover and let it cook on High for 5 minutes.

3. Stir the potatoes, cauliflower, kidney beans, tomatoes, and stock into the cooker. Season with salt and pepper, cover, and cook on Low for 6 hours.

4. When the vegetables are tender, add the coconut milk and cook, uncovered, to incorporate the flavors, 10 to 15 minutes.

Moroccan-Inspired Vegetable and Chickpea Stew

Fragrant spices and dried fruits lend a Moroccan flavor to this stew inspired by the classic tagine—a stew traditionally cooked in an earthenware pot of the same name, making it an ideal candidate for the slow cooker. Serve over couscous accompanied by a small bowl of harissa sauce (page 41) for those who like it spicy.

Slow Cooker Size:
4 to 6 quart

Cook Time: 6 to 8 hours

Setting: Low

Serves 4 to 6

1 tablespoon olive oil

3 shallots, chopped

1 large carrot, chopped

1 small yellow or red bell pepper, seeded and chopped

1 garlic clove, minced

1 teaspoon peeled and minced fresh ginger

½ teaspoon ground cinnamon

½ teaspoon ground cumin

¼ teaspoon paprika

¼ teaspoon turmeric

8 ounces green beans, ends trimmed and cut into 1-inch pieces

1½ cups slow-cooked (page 95) or one 15.5-ounce can chickpeas, drained and rinsed

One 14.5-ounce can diced tomatoes, drained and chopped

1½ cups vegetable stock (see A Note About Stock, page 32)

1 tablespoon fresh lemon juice

Salt and freshly ground black pepper

½ cup frozen peas, thawed

½ cup mixed dried fruit (apricots, apple slices, prunes, raisins, etc.), chopped

¼ cup imported green olives, drained, halved, and pitted

1 tablespoon minced fresh parsley leaves

1. In a large skillet, heat the oil over medium heat. Add the shallots, carrot, bell pepper, and garlic. Cover, and cook until softened, about 5 minutes. Add the ginger, cinnamon, cumin, paprika, and turmeric and cook, stirring, for 30 seconds to bring out the flavors.

2. Transfer the mixture to a 4- to 6-quart slow cooker. Add the green beans, chickpeas, tomatoes, stock, and lemon juice and season with salt and pepper. Cover and cook on Low for 6 to 8 hours.

3. About 20 minutes before serving, add the peas and dried fruit.

4. When ready to serve, stir in the olives and sprinkle with the parsley. Taste to adjust the seasonings and serve hot.

Veggie Jambalaya

Traditional jambalaya usually contains sausage and a variety of other meats. In this vegetarian version, feel free to add chopped seitan, tempeh, or even vegetarian pepperoni to replace all or part of the beans. Serve over hot cooked rice.

Slow Cooker Size:
4 to 6 quart

Cook Time: 6 to 8 hours

Setting: Low

Serves 4

2 tablespoons olive oil

1 large yellow onion, chopped

1 medium green bell pepper, seeded and chopped

1 celery rib, chopped

2 garlic cloves, minced

1½ cups slow-cooked (page 95) or one 15.5-ounce can dark red kidney beans, drained and rinsed

1½ cups slow-cooked (page 95) or one 15.5-ounce can black-eyed peas, drained and rinsed

One 15-ounce can crushed tomatoes

One 14.5-ounce can diced tomatoes, drained

1 cup water

1 teaspoon filé powder (optional)

¾ teaspoon dried thyme, crumbled

½ teaspoon Old Bay seasoning

Salt and freshly ground black pepper

8 ounces vegetarian sausage links, cut into 1-inch pieces

Tabasco sauce

1. Heat 1 tablespoon of the oil in a large skillet over medium heat. Add the onion, bell pepper, celery, and garlic; cover, and cook until softened, about 5 minutes.

2. Transfer to a 4- to 6-quart slow cooker. Add the beans, tomatoes, water, filé powder (if using), thyme, and Old Bay seasoning; season with salt and pepper, cover, and cook on Low for 6 to 8 hours.

3. Just before serving time, heat the remaining 1 tablespoon oil in a small skillet over medium heat. Add the sausage link pieces and cook until browned, then add to the jambalaya along with Tabasco sauce to taste.

Mediterranean Vegetable Stew

A resplendent array of vegetables from artichoke hearts to fennel permeates this delicate stew made hearty with potatoes and chickpeas. For a thicker stew, purée up to two cups of the solids at the end of the cooking time.

Slow Cooker Size:
4 to 6 quart

Cook Time: 6 to 8 hours

Setting: Low

Serves 6

2 tablespoons olive oil

3 shallots, chopped

1 large carrot, halved lengthwise and thinly sliced into half moons

2 garlic cloves, minced

1 large fennel bulb, stalks discarded, diced

1 pound small red potatoes, quartered

1 small red bell pepper, seeded and cut into 1-inch pieces

One 9-ounce package frozen artichoke hearts, thawed

One 14.5-ounce can diced tomatoes, drained

1½ cups slow-cooked (page 95) or one 15.5-ounce can chickpeas, drained and rinsed

⅓ cup dry white wine

1½ cups vegetable stock (see A Note About Stock, page 32)

1 teaspoon minced fresh thyme leaves or ¼ teaspoon dried

1 teaspoon minced fresh oregano leaves or ¼ teaspoon dried

1 large bay leaf

Salt and freshly ground black pepper

1. Heat the oil in a medium-size skillet over medium heat. Add the shallots and carrot, cover, and cook until softened, about 5 minutes. Add the garlic and cook, stirring, for 30 seconds.

2. Transfer the cooked vegetable mixture to a 4- to 6-quart slow cooker. Add the fennel, potatoes, bell pepper, artichoke hearts, tomatoes, chickpeas, wine, stock, dried thyme and oregano, if using, and bay leaf; season with salt and pepper. Cover and cook on Low for 6 to 8 hours. If using fresh herbs, add them a few minutes before the end of cooking time. Remove and discard the bay leaf before serving.

Vindaloo Vegetables

If you're looking for a way to liven up a vegetable stew, then preparing it vindaloo style may be for you. Redolent of Indian spices that are blended into a paste to bring out their flavors, this vibrant stew is delicious served over fragrant basmati rice. This version has been tamed down (vindaloo dishes are typically extremely hot), relying only on cayenne for heat that you can add at your own discretion according to your taste buds. If you really want to spike the heat, however, add one or two minced hot chiles.

Slow Cooker Size:
4 quart

Cook Time: 6 hours

Setting: Low

Serves 4

2 tablespoons olive oil

3 garlic cloves, peeled

1 tablespoon peeled and chopped fresh ginger

1 teaspoon light brown sugar

1 teaspoon ground coriander

½ teaspoon ground cumin

½ teaspoon dry mustard

½ teaspoon cayenne pepper, or to taste

½ teaspoon turmeric

1 tablespoon white wine vinegar

1 large yellow onion, chopped

2 small carrots, thinly sliced

1 small green bell pepper, seeded and diced

2 cups small cauliflower florets

2 small zucchini, cut into ¼-inch-thick slices

1½ cups slow-cooked (page 95) or one 15.5-ounce can dark red kidney beans, drained and rinsed

One 6-ounce can tomato paste blended with 1½ cups hot water

Salt and freshly ground black pepper

½ cup frozen green peas, thawed

1. In a blender or food processor, combine 1 tablespoon of the oil, the garlic, ginger, brown sugar, coriander, cumin, mustard, cayenne, turmeric, and vinegar; process until smooth, and set aside.

2. Heat the remaining 1 tablespoon oil in a medium-size skillet over medium-high heat. Add the onion and carrots, cover, and cook until softened, about 5 minutes.

3. Transfer the onion and carrot mixture to a 4-quart slow cooker and turn it on Low. Add the spice paste and cook, stirring, for 1 minute. Add the bell pepper, cauliflower, zucchini, and kidney beans. Pour in the tomato paste mixture, season with salt and pepper, cover, and cook on Low for 6 hours.

4. A few minutes before serving, stir in the peas and allow to heat through for about 10 minutes.

Vegetarian Pot au Feu

French for "pot on fire," *pot au feu* refers to a French dish of meat and vegetables slowly cooked in water. Usually, the resulting rich broth is served with croutons as a first course, followed by the meat and vegetables as a main course. The ingredients vary according to the region, so why not an all-vegetarian version? If you don't have a large slow cooker, cut down on the quantities slightly so that everything fits.

Slow Cooker Size:
5½ to 6 quart

Cook Time: 8 hours

Setting: Low

Serves 4 to 6

2 large leeks (white part only), halved lengthwise and well washed
1 pound small red potatoes, halved
2 small parsnips, peeled and sliced
2 small turnips, peeled and quartered
2 cups baby carrots
1 celery rib, cut into 2-inch pieces
1 small head green cabbage, cored and cut into 6 wedges
4 ounces green beans, ends trimmed
4 cups vegetable stock (see A Note About Stock, page 32)
1 tablespoon olive oil
Salt and freshly ground black pepper

Garnish

½ cup sour cream or tofu sour cream
2 tablespoons peeled and grated fresh horseradish
1 tablespoon Dijon mustard
1 tablespoon minced cornichons or other sour pickles
1 loaf French bread, cut into ½-inch-thick slices and toasted

1. Cut the leeks into 3-inch long pieces and place in a 5½- to 6-quart slow cooker. Add the potatoes, parsnips, turnips, carrots, celery, cabbage, and green beans. Pour the stock over all, drizzle with the olive oil, and season with salt and pepper. Cover and cook on Low for 8 hours.

2. In a small bowl, combine the sour cream, horseradish, mustard, and pickles. Set aside until ready to serve.

3. To serve, remove the vegetables from the broth. Serve the broth as a first course or alongside the entrée. Arrange the vegetables on a large platter accompanied by the horseradish sauce and toasted bread.

Slow and Easy Mushroom and Green Bean Stroganoff

Meaty mushrooms and tender green beans stand in for beef in this creamy Eastern European classic. Serve over wide noodles.

Slow Cooker Size: 4 to 6 quart

Cook Time: 6 to 8 hours

Setting: 6 to 8 hours on Low; 20 minutes on High

Serves 4

2 tablespoons olive oil
16 ounces small white mushrooms, quartered
2 tablespoons tomato paste
2 cups vegetable stock (see A Note About Stock, page 32)
1 large yellow onion, chopped
1 large green bell pepper, seeded and chopped
2 tablespoons all-purpose flour
1½ tablespoons sweet Hungarian paprika
8 ounces green beans, ends trimmed and cut into 1-inch pieces
Salt and freshly ground black pepper
½ cup sour cream or tofu sour cream

1. Heat 1 tablespoon of the oil in a large skillet over high heat. Add the mushrooms and cook quickly to brown on all sides, 3 to 4 minutes. Set aside.

2. In a small bowl, combine the tomato paste with ¼ cup of the stock, blending until smooth. Set aside.

3. Without cleaning the skillet, heat the remaining 1 tablespoon of oil over medium heat. Add the onion and bell pepper, cover, and cook until softened, about 5 minutes. Stir in the flour and cook for 1 minute to remove the raw taste.

4. Transfer the mixture to a 4- to 6-quart slow cooker. Add the paprika, green beans, the remaining 1¾ cups stock, and the tomato paste mixture; cover, and cook on Low for 6 to 8 hours.

5. At the end of cooking time, add the browned mushrooms and season with salt and pepper. Remove the cover and cook on High until the flavors are blended and the sauce thickens somewhat, about 20 minutes.

6. Just before serving, slowly whisk in the sour cream until well blended. Serve at once.

Millet and Burdock Root Stew

The sweet, earthy flavor of the firm-textured burdock root, which grows wild throughout the United States, combined with the woodsy, full-bodied flavor of the shiitake mushrooms complements the subtle creaminess of the millet. The toasted sesame oil further enhances all the flavors. Toasting the millet gives it a slightly nutty flavor. This is a pleasing, comforting stew that is especially welcome during cold winter months. Burdock is available in Asian markets and specialty grocers.

Slow Cooker Size:
4 to 6 quart

Cook Time: 6 to 8 hours

Setting: Low

Serves 4

1 cup millet
2 cups peeled and diced burdock root
1 medium-size all-purpose potato, peeled and diced
4 ounces fresh shiitake mushrooms, stemmed and caps sliced
1 teaspoon peeled and minced fresh ginger
1 tablespoon tamari or other soy sauce
1 tablespoon peanut oil
1 large yellow onion, chopped
2 medium-size carrots, diced
3 cups vegetable stock (see A Note About Stock, page 32)
1 tablespoon barley miso paste blended with 2 tablespoons hot water
1 tablespoon toasted sesame oil

1. Place the millet in a dry skillet over medium heat and cook, stirring constantly, until toasted, about 5 minutes. Be careful not to burn it.

2. Transfer the millet to a 4- to 6-quart slow cooker. Add the burdock root, potato, mushrooms, ginger, and tamari.

3. Heat the oil in a large skillet over medium heat. Add the onion and carrots, cover, and cook until softened, about 5 minutes. Add to the slow cooker along with the stock. Cover and cook on Low for 6 to 8 hours.

4. Just before serving, stir in the miso mixture and sesame oil.

Tempeh Étouffée

The word *étouffée* means "smothered"—an ideal task for the slow cooker. In this version, tempeh gets smothered by the usual vegetable trinity of South Louisiana cooking—onions, bell pepper, and celery—along with a flavorful sauce laced with thyme and marjoram. Serve over freshly cooked rice.

Slow Cooker Size:
4 quart

Cook Time: 6 to 8 hours

Setting: Low

Serves 4

2 tablespoons olive oil

12 ounces tempeh, cut into 1-inch pieces

1 medium-size yellow onion, chopped

1 celery rib, chopped

1 small green bell pepper, seeded and chopped

2 garlic cloves, minced

One 28-ounce can diced tomatoes, with their juices

1 teaspoon Tabasco sauce, or to taste

1 teaspoon salt

1½ cups water

1½ teaspoons minced fresh thyme leaves or ¾ teaspoon dried

½ teaspoon minced fresh marjoram leaves or ¼ teaspoon dried

1 tablespoon chopped fresh parsley leaves

1. Heat 1 tablespoon of the oil in a large skillet over medium heat. Add the tempeh and brown on all sides, 7 to 10 minutes. Transfer to a plate and set aside.

2. Reheat the same skillet with the remaining 1 tablespoon oil. Add the onion, celery, bell pepper, and garlic; cover, and cook until softened, about 5 minutes.

3. Transfer the vegetable mixture to a 4-quart slow cooker. Stir in the tomatoes, Tabasco, salt, and water. Add the dried thyme and marjoram, if using. Cover and cook on Low for 6 to 8 hours.

4. During the final half-hour of cooking, add the browned tempeh and the fresh thyme and marjoram, if using. Stir gently to combine. Serve hot sprinkled with the parsley.

Hungarian Goulash with Tempeh

This vegetarian version of Hungarian goulash is made with tempeh, fermented soy beans that have been compressed into a cake. Serve over wide noodles.

Slow Cooker Size: 4 quart

Cook Time: 6 hours

Setting: Low

Serves 4

2 tablespoons olive oil
1 pound tempeh, cut into ½-inch-thick slices
1 small yellow onion, halved and thinly sliced into half moons
2 cups sauerkraut, drained and rinsed
One 14.5-ounce can diced tomatoes, drained
1 tablespoon sweet Hungarian paprika
¼ cup dry white wine
1 teaspoon caraway seeds
2 tablespoons tomato paste
1½ cups vegetable stock (see A Note About Stock, page 32)
Salt and freshly ground black pepper
½ cup sour cream or tofu sour cream

1. Heat 1 tablespoon of the oil in a large skillet over medium heat. Add the tempeh and brown all over, about 10 minutes. Set aside.

2. Without cleaning the skillet, heat the remaining 1 tablespoon oil over medium heat. Add the onion, cover, and cook until softened, about 5 minutes.

3. Transfer the onions to a 4-quart slow cooker. Add the tempeh, sauerkraut, tomatoes, paprika, wine, caraway seeds, tomato paste, and stock and season with salt and pepper. Cover and cook on Low for 6 hours.

4. Just before serving, pour ½ cup of the simmering liquid into a small bowl and whisk in the sour cream. Stir this mixture back into the goulash, taste to adjust the seasonings, and serve at once.

Slow-Simmered Seitan Stifado

Seitan replaces the traditional meat in this stew inspired by the classic Greek dish made with pearl onions and seasoned with cinnamon, cloves, and oregano. Serve over hot cooked rice. If fresh pearl onions are unavailable, substitute thawed frozen pearl onions.

Slow Cooker Size:
4 quart

Cook Time: 6 to 8 hours

Setting: Low

Serves 4 to 6

8 ounces pearl onions, unpeeled

2 tablespoons olive oil

1 pound seitan, cut into 1-inch pieces

Salt and freshly ground black pepper

1 small red bell pepper, seeded and cut into ½-inch dice

2 garlic cloves, minced

One 14.5-ounce can crushed tomatoes

1 cup vegetable stock (see A Note About Stock, page 32)

¼ cup red wine vinegar

2 tablespoons tomato paste

1 teaspoon dried oregano

1 teaspoon ground cinnamon

1 teaspoon sugar

2 cloves

1 bay leaf

1. Blanch the onions in a medium-size saucepan of boiling water for 1 minute. Drain the onions, then trim the ends. To remove the peels, use a small sharp knife to cut a shallow "X" in the root end of the onions and the peels will slide off from that end. Heat 1 tablespoon of the oil in a large skillet over medium heat and add the onions. Cook until lightly browned all over, about 5 minutes, then place them in a 4-quart slow cooker.

2. Without cleaning the skillet, heat the remaining 1 tablespoon of oil over medium heat. Add the seitan and season with salt and pepper. Cook, turning once, until lightly browned, about 5 minutes, then add to the slow cooker along with the remaining ingredients. Cover and cook on low for 6 to 8 hours. Remove the bay leaf before serving.

Vegetarian Bollito Misto with Salsa Verde

This vegetarian version of *bollito misto*, literally "boiled meats," is similar to *pot au feu*—the main difference being the garnishes. Where the *pot au feu* is served with a horseradish sauce, *bollito misto* is traditionally accompanied by *salsa verde* and garnished with pickled vegetables called *giardiniera*.

Slow Cooker Size:
4 to 6 quart

Cook Time: 6 to 8 hours

Setting: Low

Serves 4

2 tablespoons olive oil
3 shallots, quartered
1 celery rib, chopped
2 garlic cloves, minced
1 pound Yukon Gold or other all-purpose potatoes, peeled and sliced
1 cup baby carrots
1 cup diced tomatoes (fresh or canned)
3 cups vegetable stock (see A Note About Stock, page 32)
2 bay leaves
Salt and freshly ground black pepper
8 ounces seitan, cut into 1-inch pieces
8 ounces vegetarian sausage links, cut into 1-inch pieces
Salsa Verde (recipe follows)

1. Heat 1 tablespoon of the oil in a large skillet over medium heat. Add the shallots, celery, and garlic, cover, and cook until softened, about 5 minutes.

2. Transfer the vegetables to a 4- to 6-quart slow cooker. Add the potatoes, carrots, tomatoes, stock, and bay leaves, season with salt and pepper, cover, and cook on Low for 6 to 8 hours.

3. About 20 minutes before you're ready to serve, heat the remaining 1 tablespoon of oil in a large skillet over medium-high heat. Add the seitan and sausage, cook until browned on all sides, about 5 minutes, then stir into the stew to finish cooking. Serve with the salsa verde.

Note: To save time when serving, brown the seitan and sausage in advance and add to the cooker during the last 15 minutes of cooking.

Salsa Verde

Flat-leaf Italian parsley is not only more traditional for this classic green herb sauce, it also has more flavor than the curly variety. If curly parsley is all you have, you can use it and the sauce will still be delicious. For a variation that tastes more like pesto, add up to ⅓ cup of fresh basil leaves or 1 teaspoon dried basil.

1 cup packed fresh Italian parsley leaves
2 tablespoons capers, drained
1 garlic clove, peeled
⅓ cup chopped pine nuts
1 tablespoon balsamic vinegar
Salt and freshly ground black pepper
½ cup extra-virgin olive oil

In a food processor or blender, combine the parsley, capers, garlic, pine nuts, vinegar, and salt and pepper to taste until smooth. With the machine running, slowly pour in the olive oil through the feed tube to achieve a smooth sauce. Taste to adjust the seasonings.

Makes about 1 cup

Wheat-Meat Cacciatore

Inspired by the popular Italian chicken dish, this "hunter's style" wheat-meat (also known as seitan), made with tomatoes, white wine, and fresh herbs, is best served over a sturdy Italian pasta, such as fettuccine.

Slow Cooker Size:
4 quart

Cook Time: 6 to 8 hours

Setting: Low

Serves 4

2 tablespoons olive oil
12 ounces seitan, cut into 1-inch pieces
½ cup dry white wine
1 small yellow onion, chopped
1 medium-size carrot, thinly sliced
1 celery rib, chopped
1 small red bell pepper, seeded and chopped
1 large garlic clove, chopped
One 14.5-ounce can diced tomatoes, with their juices
2 tablespoons tomato paste blended with 1 cup hot water
1 teaspoon minced fresh oregano leaves or ½ teaspoon dried
2 bay leaves
Salt and freshly ground black pepper

1. Heat 1 tablespoon of the oil in a medium-size skillet over medium heat. Add the seitan and cook until browned on all sides, about 5 minutes. Remove from the skillet with a slotted spoon and set aside in a bowl. Deglaze the pan with the wine, stirring to scrape up any browned bits. Simmer the wine until it reduces by half and pour on top of the seitan.

2. Without cleaning the skillet, heat the remaining 1 tablespoon of oil over medium heat. Add the onion, carrot, and celery, cover, and cook until softened, about 5 minutes.

3. Transfer the cooked vegetables to a 4-quart slow cooker. Add the bell pepper, garlic, tomatoes, tomato paste mixture, oregano, and bay leaves, and season with salt and pepper. Add the seitan and reduced wine, cover, and cook on Low for 6 to 8 hours. Remove and discard the bay leaves before serving.

Beans and Grains

. . .

Beans are an important component of veg-
etarian cooking, so it's a happy coincidence that bean
dishes are especially good when made in a
slow cooker. In fact, slow cooking is the
ideal cooking method for beans, because
what they need most to make them soft,
tender, and flavorful is long, gentle, undis-
turbed cooking.

If you follow a few simple guidelines, you can have perfectly cooked
beans every time. The most important rule is to soak your beans for several hours or overnight before cooking. This will speed the cooking
process and help to make the beans more digestible. It is also important
to wait until the beans are tender before adding salt, tomatoes, or other
acidic ingredients. These elements can toughen the beans and slow the
cooking process.

A recipe called Basic Beans (page 95) opens this chapter as a guideline
for cooking dried beans of all kinds in the slow cooker. You will find
throughout the book that many of the recipes call for slow-cooked or

canned beans. This is designed to offer the cook more flexibility. One way to combine the great flavor and economy of home-cooked beans with the convenience of canned is to cook a large batch of dried beans in the slow cooker and then portion and freeze them for later use. If you use canned beans, they should be drained and rinsed. Either way, the resulting bean dishes prepared in the slow cooker will be delicious and full of flavor.

Grains are frequently paired with beans, although grains can be somewhat temperamental when prepared in a slow cooker. Longer-cooking grains, such as wild rice, kamut, and spelt, do better than regular white or brown rice, which tends to turn out too starchy. An exception is converted rice, which does well in a slow cooker when added during the last hour of cooking. Risotto, too, can be made in a slow cooker, owing to its inherently creamy texture. Most grains, however, are best when cooked separately on top of the stove or in a rice cooker and added at the last minute or used as a bed for the slow-cooked food. A meal—slow-cooked or otherwise—that combines beans, grains, and vegetables can offer an ideally balanced food combination.

Bean Cooking Tips

- Dried beans expand when soaked and cooked—1 cup dried yields 2 to 3 cups cooked.

- If you want to prepare a recipe using dried beans, cook the beans in your slow cooker overnight. They will be done by morning and ready for you to use in recipes.

- The age of the dried beans will impact the length of cooking time.

- To help tenderize beans while adding flavor and nutrients, place a small piece of kombu sea vegetable in the pot while the beans cook.

- Dried herbs should be added to beans during the final 30 minutes of cooking time. However, it is best to add fresh herbs after the beans are cooked for the best flavor.

- To keep cooked beans from drying out, cool them in their cooking water.

- For future convenience, cook a large amount of beans, then portion and freeze them.

- Once cooked, beans will keep in the refrigerator for up to a week if kept in a tightly sealed container. They can be stored in the freezer for three to six months.

- For improved digestibility when cooking beans, be sure to drain the cooking water first before using the cooked beans in a recipe.

Basic Beans

Use this recipe as a guideline to slow cook basic dried beans such as pintos, kidneys, white beans, and black-eyed peas. If you want to flavor the beans, you can add the onion, garlic, and bay leaves. If you prefer them "as is," just cook them in water and you will have beans that are ready to use in any kind of recipe calling for cooked beans.

Slow Cooker Size:
5½ to 6 quart

Cook Time: 8 to 12
hours or more

Setting: High

Makes 5 to 6 cups

1 pound dried beans, picked over and rinsed
1 large yellow onion, quartered (optional)
2 garlic cloves, crushed (optional)
2 bay leaves (optional)

1. Soak the beans in enough water to cover plus an inch or two for 8 hours or overnight.

2. Drain the beans and place them in a 5½- to 6-quart slow cooker. Add the onion, garlic, and bay leaves, if using, and enough water to cover (6 to 8 cups). Cover and cook on High for 8 to 12 hours, or longer, depending on the type of bean.

Bean Business

There are more than 13,000 known varieties of beans and legumes in the world, although most of us are familiar with no more than a dozen. Below is a list of the most commonly used beans that can be cooked in a slow cooker.

Adzuki beans

Black beans

Black-eyed peas

Cannellini beans

Chickpeas

Great Northern beans

Kidney beans

Lima beans

Navy beans

Pinto beans

While most beans will be done cooking in 8 to 12 hours, some may take up to 16 hours, depending on the age and variety of bean.

Note: Lentils and split peas do not require soaking and will usually be tender within 6 hours.

Magic Beans

Like magic, plain cooked "basic beans" can be transformed into a delicious meal with a few simple additions. For better digestibility, drain the Basic Beans before proceeding, then add some or all of the ingredients in any of these four variations to a pot of Basic Beans.

Southwest Beans

1 recipe Basic Beans (page 95)
One 4-ounce can chopped green chiles, drained
1 teaspoon ground cumin
1 teaspoon paprika
Salt and freshly ground black pepper

Drain the cooking liquid from the beans, then stir in the chiles, cumin, and paprika, and season with salt and pepper. Reduce the heat setting to Low, cover, and cook for 30 minutes to blend the flavors. Add some water or stock if you prefer a saucier consistency.

Asian-Flavor Beans

1 recipe Basic Beans (page 95), kept warm
2 tablespoons tamari or other soy sauce
2 scallions, minced
1 tablespoon toasted sesame oil

Just before serving, drain the beans and stir in the tamari, scallions, and sesame oil.

Mediterranean Beans

1 recipe Basic Beans (page 95), kept warm
1 tablespoon olive oil
2 garlic cloves, minced
¼ cup pesto, homemade (page 51) or store-bought
¼ cup sun-dried tomatoes, soaked in hot water to cover until softened,
    drained, and chopped

Just before serving, heat the oil in a small skillet, add the garlic, and cook until fragrant, about 30 seconds. Stir in the pesto and tomatoes. Drain the beans, then stir in the pesto mixture.

Very Veggie Beans

1 recipe Basic Beans (page 95), kept warm
⅓ cup fresh or frozen corn kernels, cooked until tender in boiling water
    and drained
⅓ cup chopped roasted red bell pepper
⅓ cup chopped fresh tomato
1 teaspoon Liquid Smoke (optional)
Salt and freshly ground black pepper

Shortly before serving, drain the beans, then stir in the corn kernels, roasted bell pepper, tomato, and Liquid Smoke, if using. Season with salt and pepper.

Maple Baked Beans

With a slow cooker, you can recreate the old-fashioned goodness of baked beans when they were simmered for hours in a ceramic bean pot not unlike the insert of a slow cooker. The natural sweetness of pure maple syrup adds to the great flavor.

Slow Cooker Size:
3½ to 4 quart

Cook Time: 6 to 8 hours

Setting: Low

Serves 4

1 tablespoon olive oil

1 medium-size yellow onion, chopped

3 cups slow-cooked (page 95) or two 15.5-ounce cans navy beans or Great Northern beans, drained and rinsed

½ cup pure maple syrup

1 teaspoon dry mustard

½ teaspoon salt

¼ teaspoon freshly ground black pepper

¼ cup tomato paste mixed with 1¼ cups hot water

1. Heat the oil in a large skillet over medium heat. Add the onion, cover, and cook until softened, about 5 minutes.

2. Transfer the onion to a 3½- to 4-quart slow cooker. Add the beans, maple syrup, mustard, salt, and pepper. Pour in the tomato paste mixture, cover, and cook on Low for 6 to 8 hours.

Orange and Bourbon Baked Beans

Everyday baked beans take on a sophisticated character with the addition of bourbon and orange juice.

Slow Cooker Size:
3½ to 4 quart

Cook Time: 4 to 6 hours

Setting: Low

Serves 4

1 tablespoon olive oil
1 large yellow onion, chopped
One 14.5-ounce can crushed tomatoes
¼ cup molasses
2 tablespoons cider vinegar
1 tablespoon prepared mustard
1 tablespoon tamari or other soy sauce
3 cups slow-cooked (page 95) or two 15.5-ounce cans navy beans or other white beans, drained and rinsed
¼ cup bourbon
¼ cup frozen orange juice concentrate

1. Heat the oil in a medium-size skillet over medium heat. Add the onion, cover, and cook until softened, about 5 minutes.

2. Transfer the onions to a 3½- to 4-quart slow cooker. Add the tomatoes, molasses, vinegar, mustard, and tamari, stirring to combine. Stir in the beans, bourbon, and orange juice concentrate, cover, and cook on Low for 4 to 6 hours.

Using the Old Bean

If you want to prepare a recipe using dried beans, cook the beans first in your slow cooker overnight. They will be done by morning and ready for you to use in recipes.

Slow and Easy White Bean Cassoulet

White beans are an essential part of any classic French cassoulet and here they take center stage as they slowly simmer with vegetables and herbs. The optional tempeh confit introduces another flavor element. Instead of the confit, you can add lightly browned pieces of vegetarian sausage links, if you like. Crusty French bread is an ideal accompaniment.

Slow Cooker Size:
4 quart

Cook Time: 8 hours

Setting: Low

Serves 4 to 6

2 tablespoons olive oil

1 large sweet yellow onion, chopped

8 ounces baby carrots, halved

2 garlic cloves, minced

3 cups slow-cooked (page 95) or two 15.5-ounce cans Great Northern or other white beans, drained and rinsed

One 28-ounce can diced tomatoes, with their juices

1 tablespoon tomato paste

½ cup vegetable stock (see A Note on Stock, page 32)

¼ cup white wine

2 bay leaves

1 teaspoon dried thyme

Salt and freshly ground black pepper

½ cup dry bread crumbs

1½ cups Tempeh and Shallot Confit (page 22; optional)

1 tablespoon chopped fresh parsley leaves

1. Heat 1 tablespoon of the oil in a large skillet over medium heat. Add the onion, carrots, and garlic, cover, and cook until softened, about 5 minutes.

2. Transfer the onion mixture to a 4-quart slow cooker. Add the beans, tomatoes, tomato paste, stock, wine, bay leaves, and thyme; season with salt and pepper, cover, and cook on Low for 8 hours.

3. While the cassoulet is cooking, lightly toast the bread crumbs in a small skillet with the remaining 1 tablespoon oil over medium-high heat.

4. When the cassoulet is ready to serve, remove and discard the bay leaves, stir in the tempeh confit, if using, and top with the crumbs. Serve hot, garnished with the parsley.

What a Dal

Aromatic spices turn everyday beans and lentils into an exotic dish with the flavors of India. If a smoother texture is desired, purée up to two cups of the finished product in a blender or food processor and stir back into the pot. Serve over freshly cooked basmati rice.

Slow Cooker Size:
4 quart

Cook Time: 8 hours

Setting: Low

Serves 6

2 tablespoons olive oil
1 large yellow onion, cut into pieces
2 garlic cloves, peeled
1 teaspoon peeled and minced fresh ginger
1 teaspoon ground coriander
1 teaspoon ground cumin
1 teaspoon turmeric
½ teaspoon ground cardamom
½ teaspoon dry mustard
¼ teaspoon cayenne pepper
¼ teaspoon ground allspice
1½ cups dried brown lentils, picked over and rinsed
1½ cups slow-cooked (page 95) or one 15.5-ounce can kidney beans, drained and rinsed
3 cups water
Salt and freshly ground black pepper

1. Pour the oil into a 4-quart slow cooker and set it on High.

2. In a food processor, purée the onion, garlic, and ginger and add it to the cooker. Cover and cook to mellow the flavor and remove the raw taste while you assemble the other ingredients. Stir in the coriander, cumin, turmeric, cardamom, mustard, cayenne, and allspice, and cook, stirring, for 30 seconds.

3. Turn the setting to Low. Add the lentils, kidney beans, and water; cover, and cook for 8 hours. Before serving, season with salt and pepper and adjust the other seasonings if necessary.

Sloppy Lentils

Meaty lentils are featured in this vegetarian version of Sloppy Joes. Serve on toasted rolls with a fresh batch of coleslaw.

Slow Cooker Size:
3½ to 4 quart

Cook Time: 8 hours

Setting: Low

Serves 4 to 6

1 tablespoon olive oil
1 medium-size yellow onion, chopped
1 small red or green bell pepper, seeded and chopped
1 tablespoon chili powder
1½ cups dried brown lentils, picked over and rinsed
One 14.5-ounce can crushed tomatoes
3 cups water
2 tablespoons tamari or other soy sauce
1 tablespoon prepared mustard
1 tablespoon light brown sugar or a natural sweetener
1 teaspoon salt
Freshly ground black pepper

1. Heat the oil in a medium-size skillet over medium heat. Add the onion and bell pepper, cover, and cook until softened, about 5 minutes. Add the chili powder, stirring to coat.

2. Transfer the onion mixture to a 3½- to 4-quart slow cooker. Add the lentils, tomatoes, water, tamari, mustard, brown sugar, salt, and pepper to taste and stir to combine. Cover and cook on Low for 8 hours.

Pintos Picadillo

Pinto beans replace the traditional ground beef in this vibrant Mexican dish that is at once sweet, spicy, hot, and piquant.

Slow Cooker Size:
3½ to 4 quart

Cook Time: 6 to 8 hours

Setting: Low

Serves 4

1 tablespoon olive oil

1 medium-size yellow onion, chopped

1 small red bell pepper, seeded and chopped

2 garlic cloves, minced

3 cups slow-cooked (page 95) or two 15.5-ounce cans pinto beans, drained and rinsed

One 14.5-ounce can diced tomatoes, drained

One 4-ounce can diced green chiles, drained

1 Granny Smith apple, peeled, cored, and chopped

1 cup vegetable stock (see A Note About Stock, page 32)

Salt and freshly ground black pepper

2 cups cooked long-grain white or brown rice

½ cup golden raisins

¼ cup sliced black olives, drained

2 tablespoons chopped fresh parsley leaves

2 tablespoons slivered almonds, toasted (page 185)

1. Heat the oil in a large skillet over medium heat. Add the onion and bell pepper, cover, and cook until softened, about 5 minutes.

2. Transfer the vegetables to a 3½- to 4-quart slow cooker. Add the garlic, beans, tomatoes, chiles, apple, and stock; season with salt and pepper, cover, and cook on Low for 6 to 8 hours.

3. About 10 minutes before serving, stir in the rice, raisins, olives, parsley, and almonds.

Spicy Black Beans and Rice with Mangoes

Fresh mangoes add a burst of color, texture, and sweetness to these spicy black beans and rice with a Caribbean flavor.

Slow Cooker Size:
3½ to 4 quart

Cook Time: 6 to 8 hours

Setting: Low

Serves 4 to 6

1 tablespoon olive oil
1 small yellow onion, finely chopped
½ red bell pepper, seeded and chopped
2 garlic cloves, minced
1 jalapeño or other hot chile, seeded and minced
½ teaspoon peeled and minced fresh ginger
½ teaspoon ground cumin
½ teaspoon ground allspice
¼ teaspoon dried oregano
3 cups slow-cooked (page 95) or two 15.5-ounce can black beans, drained and rinsed
1 cup water
½ teaspoon light brown sugar or a natural sweetener
½ teaspoon salt
¼ teaspoon freshly ground black pepper
3 cups cooked long-grain white rice
2 medium-size ripe mangoes, peeled, flesh cut away from the seed, and diced

1. Heat the oil in a large skillet over medium heat. Add the onion, bell pepper, garlic, and jalapeño, cover, and cook until softened, about 5 minutes. Stir in the ginger, cumin, allspice, and oregano and cook for 1 minute to bring out their flavor.

2. Transfer the sautéed mixture to a 3½- to 4-quart slow cooker. Stir in the beans, water, brown sugar, salt, and pepper; cover, and cook on Low for 6 to 8 hours.

3. Taste to adjust the seasonings before serving. About 10 minutes before serving, stir in the rice and mangoes.

Slow Spanish Beans and Rice

Flavorful and nutritious brown rice is cooked ahead of time and added near the end of the cooking time so that the grains remain separate and fluffy—most rice tends to get gummy and starchy when cooked directly in a slow cooker. If you prefer to cook your rice right in the slow cooker, you will get the best results by adding one cup of converted white rice about an hour before the end of cooking time and increasing the water by one cup.

Slow Cooker Size:
3½ to 4 quart

Cook Time: 6 to 8 hours

Setting: Low

Serves 4

1 tablespoon olive oil
1 medium-size yellow onion, chopped
1 small red or green bell pepper, seeded and chopped
2 garlic cloves, minced
¼ cup tomato paste
2 teaspoons chili powder
3 cups slow-cooked (page 95) or two 15.5-ounce cans pinto or kidney beans, drained and rinsed
One 14.5-ounce can diced tomatoes, with their juices
1½ cups water
1 tablespoon tamari or other soy sauce
Salt and freshly ground black pepper
3 cups cooked long-grain brown rice

1. Heat the oil in a medium-size skillet over medium heat. Add the onion, bell pepper, and garlic, cover, and cook until softened, about 5 minutes. Add the tomato paste and chili powder and stir to coat.

2. Transfer the onion mixture to a 3½- to 4-quart slow cooker. Add the beans, tomatoes, water, and tamari; season with salt and pepper, cover, and cook on Low for 6 to 8 hours.

3. About 10 minutes before serving time, stir in the rice.

Vegetarian Hoppin' John

Hoppin' John has been a New Year's tradition in my house since the mid-1980s when I lived in Charleston, South Carolina, and discovered its good taste and promise of good fortune for the coming year. Brown rice is more nutritious than white, but you can use white if you like. To cut down on last-minute prep time, cook the rice and brown the sausage the day before.

Slow Cooker Size:
3½ to 4 quart

Cook Time: 4 to 6 hours

Setting: Low

Serves 4 to 6

2 tablespoons olive oil
1 medium-size yellow onion, chopped
1 celery rib, chopped
3 garlic cloves, minced
1 teaspoon dried thyme
3 cups slow-cooked (page 95) or two 15.5-ounce cans black-eyed peas, drained and rinsed
One 14.5-ounce can tomatoes, drained and finely chopped
One 4-ounce can diced green chiles, drained
1 cup vegetable stock (see A Note About Stock, page 32)
Salt and freshly ground black pepper
8 ounces vegetarian sausage, crumbled
3 cups cooked long-grain brown or white rice (see Note below)

1. Heat 1 tablespoon of the oil in a medium-size skillet over medium heat. Add the onion and celery, cover, and cook until softened, about 5 minutes. Add the garlic and thyme, stirring to bring out their flavors.

2. Transfer to a 3½- to 4-quart slow cooker. Add the black-eyed peas, tomatoes, chiles, and stock, season with salt and pepper, cover, and cook on Low for 4 to 6 hours.

3. About 15 minutes before serving, heat the remaining 1 tablespoon oil in a medium-size skillet over medium heat. Cook the sausage until browned all over, about 8 minutes. Add the sausage to the slow cooker along with the rice, stirring to combine. Taste to adjust the seasonings.

Note: If you want to cook your rice directly in the slow cooker with the black-eyed peas, you will need to use converted rice. (Brown rice and regular while rice become too starchy.) To do this, add 1 cup converted rice to the cooker 1 hour before serving time. You may also need to add up to 1 cup water or stock, because the uncooked rice will absorb the liquid as it cooks and it may become too dry.

Wild Rice Pilaf with Peas, Lemon Zest, and Tarragon

Wild rice and brown rice combine in this pilaf that is lightened up with the fresh taste of lemon, tarragon, and sweet green peas. Wild rice does well in a slow cooker, but brown rice tends to get mushy, so it is cooked separately and added near the end of the cooking time.

Slow Cooker Size:
3½ to 4 quart

Cook Time: 5 to 6 hours

Setting: Low

Serves 4

2 tablespoons olive oil
3 shallots, finely chopped
1 cup wild rice
3 cups vegetable stock (see A Note About Stock, page 32)
Salt and freshly ground black pepper
3 cups cooked long-grain brown rice
⅔ cup frozen baby peas, thawed
Juice and grated zest of 1 lemon
1 tablespoon chopped fresh tarragon leaves

1. Heat the oil in a small skillet over medium heat. Add the shallots, cover, and cook until softened, about 5 minutes.

2. Transfer the sautéed shallots to a 3½- to 4-quart slow cooker. Stir in the wild rice and stock, season with salt and pepper, cover, and cook on Low for 5 to 6 hours.

3. About 10 minutes before serving, stir in the brown rice, peas, lemon juice and zest, and tarragon. Taste to adjust the seasonings and serve.

Wild Mushroom Risotto

Fresh and dried mushrooms combine for a woodsy mushroom-flavored risotto that needs no watching or constant stirring like traditional risottos. Instead, you can spend your time shopping, soaking in the tub, or reading a good book.

Slow Cooker Size:
3½ to 4 quart

Cook Time: 2 hours

Setting: High

Serves 4

¼ cup dried porcini mushrooms
1 cup boiling water
3 tablespoons olive oil
2 shallots, minced
1 large garlic clove, minced
1¼ cups arborio rice
2 cups chopped cremini mushrooms
2½ cups vegetable stock (see A Note About Stock, page 32)
¼ cup white wine
2 teaspoons chopped fresh thyme leaves or 1 teaspoon dried
1 teaspoon salt
½ cup freshly grated Parmesan cheese or soy Parmesan
1 tablespoon minced fresh parsley leaves
Freshly ground black pepper

1. Soak the dried porcini in the boiling water for 30 minutes. Drain, reserving ¾ cup of the soaking liquid. Chop the mushrooms and set aside.

2. In a medium-size skillet, heat the oil over medium heat. Add the shallots and garlic and cook until fragrant and slightly softened, about 1 minute.

3. Transfer the shallots and garlic to a 3½- to 4-quart slow cooker. Add the rice, stirring to coat it with oil. Stir in all the mushrooms, the reserved soaking liquid, stock, wine, thyme, and salt; cover, and cook on High for about 2 hours, until all liquid is absorbed.

4. About 5 minutes before the risotto is finished, stir in the cheese and parsley and season with pepper. To serve, spoon the risotto into shallow bowls and serve hot.

White Beans and Spelt with Escarole

Spelt, also known as farro, is a member of the wheat family that is more widely used in Europe than in the United States. In combination with white beans and escarole, it is a typically Tuscan dish. Since spelt is a large grain that requires a lengthy cooking time, it is a good candidate for the slow cooker. Look for spelt in natural food stores.

Slow Cooker Size:
3½ to 4 quart

Cook Time: 8 hours

Setting: Low

Serves 4

1 large head escarole, coarsely chopped
1 cup spelt, soaked in water for 4 hours or overnight and drained
3 cups vegetable stock (see A Note About Stock, page 32)
Salt and freshly ground black pepper
2 tablespoons olive oil
3 garlic cloves, finely minced
1½ cups slow-cooked (page 95) or one 15.5-ounce can cannellini or other white beans, drained and rinsed

1. Cook the escarole in a pot of boiling salted water for 5 minutes. Drain well and set aside.

2. Place the spelt in a 3½- to 4-quart slow cooker, stir in the stock, and season with salt and pepper. Cover, and cook on Low for 8 hours, until the spelt is tender.

3. Heat the oil in a large skillet over medium heat. Add the garlic and cook until fragrant, about 30 seconds. Add the escarole and cook until tender, stirring occasionally, about 5 minutes. Add the beans and season with salt and pepper to taste. Set aside.

4. About 20 minutes before serving time, add the escarole and bean mixture to the slow cooker and stir gently to combine. Cover and let simmer so the flavors can mingle.

Garlicky Polenta with Wild Mushroom Sauté

Polenta is easy in the slow cooker because it doesn't require all the stirring and close watching that is necessary in the stove-top method. Garlic is added to the polenta and the mushrooms so that its flavor permeates the entire dish. Regular white button mushrooms may be added to the mushroom assortment if you like.

Slow Cooker Size:
3½ to 4 quart

Cook Time: 6 to 8 hours

Setting: Low

Serves 6 to 8

Polenta

1 tablespoon olive oil
1 garlic clove, minced
6 cups boiling water
1 teaspoon salt
2 cups medium- or coarse-ground cornmeal

Mushrooms

2 tablespoons olive oil
1 garlic clove, minced
8 ounces assorted fresh cremini, shiitake, and oyster mushrooms, stems trimmed or removed and sliced
Salt and freshly ground black pepper

1. To make the polenta, lightly oil the insert of a 3½- to 4-quart slow cooker. Add the olive oil and garlic and turn the cooker to High. Carefully pour in the boiling water and salt, then slowly whisk in the cornmeal, stirring constantly until blended. Cover and cook on Low for 6 to 8 hours, stirring occasionally.

2. Spoon the cooked polenta into a lightly oiled loaf pan and smooth the top. Refrigerate until firm, 30 to 40 minutes.

3. To make the mushrooms, heat 1 tablespoon of the olive oil in a medium-size skillet over medium heat. Add the garlic and cook until fragrant, about 30 seconds. Add the mushrooms and cook until tender, about 5 minutes, stirring a few times. Season with salt and pepper and keep warm over very low heat.

4. Preheat the oven to 375°F. Cut the firm polenta into ½-inch-thick slices and place them on a lightly oiled baking sheet. Brush the top of the polenta slices with the remaining 1 tablespoon olive oil and bake until hot and golden brown, 20 to 30 minutes.

5. To serve, arrange the polenta slices on a serving platter and spoon the mushrooms on top. Serve hot.

Note: Because this dish needs additional time to prepare (30 minutes in the refrigerator, then 30 minutes in the oven), it may be more convenient to make the polenta overnight, then you can refrigerate it before going to work and it will be ready to pop in the oven when you get home.

Kamut with Root Vegetables and Cranberries

Slow cooking is a good way to prepare kamut, a large wheat-like grain that requires a long slow simmer to soften. Look for kamut in natural food stores. The addition of root vegetables and cranberries give this dish a decidedly winter feel.

Slow Cooker Size:
4 quart

Cook Time: 8 to 9 hours

Setting: Low

Serves 6

2 tablespoons olive oil
2 large shallots, minced
1 cup kamut, soaked in water for 4 hours or overnight and drained
1 large carrot, chopped
1 medium-size parsnip, peeled and chopped
1 small celery root, peeled and shredded
3 cups boiling vegetable stock (see A Note About Stock, page 32) or water
Salt and freshly ground black pepper
½ cup sweetened dried cranberries
2 tablespoons minced fresh parsley leaves

1. Pour the oil into a 4-quart slow cooker and turn the setting to High. Add the shallots, cover, and cook until softened slightly.

2. Add the kamut, carrot, parsnip, and celery root to the slow cooker, stir in the stock, and season with salt and pepper. Cover and cook on Low for 8 to 9 hours.

3. A few minutes before serving, stir in the cranberries and taste to adjust the seasonings. Sprinkle with the parsley and serve.

Potpies, Pastas, and Other Main Dishes

• • •

While bean soups and chili may be the darlings of a vegetarian's slow cooker repertoire, a multitude of other main dishes deserve attention as well.

Some of the recipes in this chapter are vegetarian versions of classic international dishes that lend themselves to slow cooking, such as Moroccan tagine, Indian curry, and even good old American pot roast. Many of these recipes would traditionally call for meat, which the slow-cooking process helps to make tender. When these recipes are meatless, however, slow cooking is employed not to tenderize, but for the sheer convenience and enriched flavor that long, gentle cooking can bring to the ingredients.

This chapter also includes uniquely vegetarian recipes for braising tofu and making seitan (wheat-meat) from scratch. In addition, there are recipes for lasagna, potpies, and other casseroles—dishes usually associated with oven baking—which serve to further illustrate the versatility of the slow cooker.

Farmhouse Fricassee

A fricassee usually describes a dish of chicken or other meat that has been stewed with vegetables, but the ingredients are usually cut into larger pieces than they are for a stew. In this recipe, a variety of farm-fresh vegetables are used, but feel free to substitute other vegetables that are in season or on hand. Your choice of tempeh or seitan can be used.

Slow Cooker Size:
4 to 6 quart

Cook Time: 8 hours

Setting: Low

Serves 4

2 tablespoons olive oil
4 shallots, quartered
½ cup dry white wine
12 ounces seitan or tempeh, cut into ½-inch-thick slices
8 ounces baby carrots, halved lengthwise
8 ounces small red potatoes, halved
8 ounces green beans, ends trimmed and cut into 1-inch pieces
One 14.5-ounce can diced tomatoes, drained
1½ cups vegetable stock (see A Note About Stock, page 32)
Salt and freshly ground black pepper
1 tablespoon minced fresh tarragon or parsley leaves

1. Heat 1 tablespoon of the oil in a large skillet over medium heat. Add the shallots, cover, and cook until softened, about 5 minutes. Add the wine and cook for 1 minute to reduce slightly. Transfer the shallot mixture to a 4- to 6-quart slow cooker.

2. Heat the remaining 1 tablespoon oil in the same skillet over medium heat. Add the seitan or tempeh and cook until browned on both sides, about 10 minutes, then add to the slow cooker along with the carrots, potatoes, green beans, tomatoes, and stock; season with salt and pepper. Stir to combine, cover, and cook on Low for 8 hours.

3. Just before serving, stir in the tarragon.

Miso-Braised Tofu and Shallots

As a rule, tofu doesn't stand up well to slow cooking, but it does just fine when braised in a small amount of liquid, as in this recipe. Here, slow cooking draws out the water content of the tofu and allows the flavorful miso sauce to soak in. This recipe works best in a wide, shallow slow cooker so that you can arrange more of the tofu in a single layer.

Slow Cooker Size:
4 quart (or larger)

Cook Time: 4 hours

Setting: Low

Serves 4

3 shallots, thinly sliced
1 pound extra-firm tofu, drained
2 tablespoons miso paste
2 tablespoons tamari or other soy sauce
1 tablespoon olive oil
1 tablespoon water

1. Spread the shallots over the bottom of a lightly oiled 4-quart (or larger) slow cooker. Cut the tofu into ½-inch-thick slabs and arrange in layers on top of the shallots.

2. In a small bowl, combine the miso paste, tamari, oil, and water, and pour over the tofu and shallots. Cover and cook on Low for about 4 hours.

Why I Love My Slow Cooker

1. It has dinner ready and waiting for me at the end of the day.

2. It frees up burners when I need them the most—at holidays and party time.

3. It performs as a chafing dish or an electric punch bowl at parties.

4. It keeps my kitchen cool on hot days.

5. I can cook and serve in the same container so it saves time when cleaning up.

Five-Layer Vegetable Strata with Pesto

Layers of vegetables cook together slowly, their flavors united by a pesto-infused white bean purée, which makes a rich sauce. Vary the vegetables according to taste. Browning the potatoes and onions in advance is worth the time because it adds color and flavor to the dish.

Slow Cooker Size:
3½ to 4 quart

Cook Time: 6 to 8 hours

Setting: Low

Serves 4

1½ cups slow-cooked (page 95) or one 15.5-ounce can cannellini or other white beans, drained and rinsed
1 cup vegetable stock (see A Note About Stock, page 32)
2 tablespoons pesto, homemade (page 51) or store-bought
1 tablespoon olive oil
2 large Yukon Gold potatoes, peeled and thinly sliced
1 large yellow onion, cut in half and thinly sliced into half moons
Salt and freshly ground black pepper
1 medium-size red bell pepper, seeded and thinly sliced into rings
1 large zucchini, thinly sliced
1 large ripe tomato, thinly sliced

1. In a food processor or blender, process the beans, stock, and pesto together until well blended. Set aside.

2. Heat the oil in a large skillet over medium-high heat. Add the potato slices and cook, turning once, until golden brown on both sides, about 10 minutes. Set aside. Add the onion slices to the same pan and cook until browned on both sides, about 5 minutes. Set aside.

3. Lightly oil the insert of a 3½- to 4-quart slow cooker. Spooning a small amount of the bean mixture between each layer of vegetables, layer the potato slices and season with salt and pepper. Top with the onions, followed by the bean mixture, bell pepper slices, more bean mixture, zucchini slices, more bean mixture, and tomato. Pour the remaining bean mixture over all. Cover and cook on Low for 6 to 8 hours.

Tempeh Choucroute Garnie

Tempeh and vegetarian sausage links are used to garnish the sauerkraut in this robust dish redolent of caraway and juniper berries. Dried juniper berries (and caraway seeds) are available in the spice section of well-stocked supermarkets or gourmet grocers.

Slow Cooker Size:
3½ to 4 quart

Cook Time: 6 to 8 hours

Setting: Low

Serves 4

2 tablespoons olive oil

8 ounces tempeh, cut into ½-inch-thick strips

8 ounces vegetarian sausage links

1 medium-size yellow onion, chopped

12 ounces small white potatoes, halved or quartered

2 cups sauerkraut, drained and rinsed

½ cup Riesling or other white wine

1 teaspoon sweet Hungarian paprika

½ teaspoon caraway seeds

½ teaspoon juniper berries

1 cup vegetable stock (see A Note About Stock, page 32)

Salt and freshly ground black pepper

1. Heat the oil in a large skillet over medium heat. Add the tempeh and cook until browned all over, 5 to 7 minutes. Remove the tempeh with a slotted spoon and set aside. Add the vegetarian sausage links to the same skillet and cook until browned all over, about 5 minutes. Remove the links with a slotted spoon and set aside with the tempeh.

2. Reheat the same skillet over medium heat, adding a little more oil if necessary. Add the onion, cover, and cook until softened, about 5 minutes.

3. Transfer the onion to a 3½- to 4-quart slow cooker. Add the potatoes, sauerkraut, wine, paprika, caraway seeds, and juniper berries. Pour in the stock, season with salt and pepper, cover, and cook on Low for 6 to 8 hours.

4. About 20 minutes before serving time, add the tempeh and vegetarian sausage links to the cooker and stir gently to combine.

Arroz non Pollo

Slow cooking helps to deepen and enrich the flavors of this vegetarian version of *arroz con pollo* that tastes like the Spanish classic—but made with chickpeas instead of chicken. If you want to make this recipe with regular white or brown rice, cook the rice separately and add to the slow cooker near the end of the cooking time. You will also need to reduce the amount of stock in the recipe by one cup. Turmeric may be substituted for the saffron to add color.

Slow Cooker Size:
4 to 6 quart

Cook Time: 6 to 8 hours
(rice added during last
hour of cooking)

Setting: Low

Serves 4

1 tablespoon olive oil
1 medium-size yellow onion, chopped
1 small carrot, chopped
2 garlic cloves, chopped
½ teaspoon dried oregano
½ teaspoon ground cumin
⅛ teaspoon saffron threads
One 14.5-ounce can diced tomatoes, with their juices
3 cups vegetable stock (see A Note About Stock, page 32)
1 small red bell pepper, seeded and chopped
8 ounces green beans, ends trimmed and cut into 1-inch lengths
1½ cups slow-cooked (page 95) or one 15.5-ounce can chickpeas, drained and rinsed
Salt and freshly ground black pepper
1 cup converted or Valencia rice
¾ cup salsa of your choice
½ cup frozen peas, thawed
⅓ cup sliced pimiento-stuffed green olives, drained

1. Heat the oil in a large skillet over medium heat. Add the onion and carrot, cover, and cook until softened, about 5 minutes. Stir in the garlic, oregano, cumin, and saffron and cook for 2 minutes longer.

2. Transfer the vegetable mixture to a lightly oiled 4- to 6-quart slow cooker. Add the tomatoes, stock, bell pepper, green beans, and chickpeas; season with salt and pepper, cover, and cook on Low for 6 to 8 hours.

3. About an hour before the end of cooking time, stir in the rice, cover, and cook on Low until tender.

4. About 10 minutes before serving, stir in the salsa, peas, and olives, and cover. Taste to adjust the seasonings before serving.

Vegetarian Paella

Instead of meat and seafood, this vegetarian version of paella relies on kidney beans, oyster mushrooms, and vegetarian sausage to combine with the flavorful vegetables and rice. Converted rice is used in this recipe to produce firm, separate grains. If you use Valencia rice, which is traditional to paella, the results will be creamier.

Slow Cooker Size:
5½ to 6 quart

Cook Time: 5 hours
(rice added during last
hour of cooking)

Setting: Low

Serves 4 to 6

2 tablespoons olive oil

1 medium-size yellow onion, chopped

1 small green bell pepper, seeded and diced

4 ounces green beans, ends trimmed and cut into 1-inch pieces

One 28-ounce can whole plum tomatoes, drained and chopped

2 garlic cloves, minced

One 9-ounce package frozen artichoke hearts, thawed

1½ cups slow-cooked (page 95) or one 15.5-ounce can dark red kidney beans, drained and rinsed

3 cups vegetable stock (see A Note About Stock, page 32)

½ teaspoon red pepper flakes

¼ teaspoon saffron threads

2 bay leaves

Salt and freshly ground black pepper

1 cup converted white rice or Valencia rice

8 ounces vegetarian sausage links, cut into 1-inch pieces

4 ounces oyster mushrooms, stems trimmed and cut into 1-inch pieces

1 cup frozen peas, thawed

1 tablespoon minced fresh parsley leaves

1 lemon, cut into 4 to 6 wedges

1. Heat 1 tablespoon of the oil in a medium-size skillet over medium heat. Add the onion, cover, and cook until softened, about 5 minutes.

2. Transfer the onion to a $5\frac{1}{2}$- to 6-quart slow cooker. Stir in the bell pepper, green beans, tomatoes, garlic, artichoke hearts, kidney beans, stock, pepper flakes, saffron, and bay leaves and season with salt and black pepper. Cover, and cook on Low for 4 hours.

3. Stir in the rice, cover, and cook on Low for another hour, until the rice is tender.

4. Meanwhile, heat the remaining 1 tablespoon oil in a medium-size skillet over medium heat. Add the sausage links and cook until browned, about 5 minutes. Remove from the pan and set aside. Add the oyster mushrooms to the same pan and cook, stirring, until tender, about 3 minutes.

5. About 10 minutes before ready to serve, stir the sausage links, oyster mushrooms, and peas into the paella. Cover and finish cooking. Serve garnished with the parsley and lemon wedges.

No Hurry Vegetable Curry

Let the luscious fragrance of curry fill your house all day as it simmers in your slow cooker. Serve over hot cooked basmati rice with chutney on the side.

Slow Cooker Size:
3½ to 4 quart

Cook Time: 6 to 8 hours

Setting: Low

Serves 4

1 tablespoon peanut oil
2 large carrots, sliced on a diagonal
1 medium-size yellow onion, chopped
3 garlic cloves, minced
2 tablespoons curry powder
1 teaspoon ground coriander
¼ teaspoon cayenne pepper
2 large Yukon Gold potatoes, peeled and diced
8 ounces green beans, ends trimmed and cut into 1-inch pieces
1½ cups slow-cooked (page 95) or one 15.5-ounce can chickpeas, drained and rinsed
One 14.5-ounce can diced tomatoes, drained
2 cups vegetable stock (see A Note About Stock, page 32)
½ cup frozen green peas, thawed
½ cup canned unsweetened coconut milk
Salt

1. Heat the oil in a large skillet over medium heat. Add the carrots and onion, cover, and cook until softened, about 5 minutes. Add the garlic, curry powder, coriander, and cayenne, stirring to coat.

2. Transfer the vegetable mixture to a 3½- to 4-quart slow cooker. Add the potatoes, green beans, chickpeas, tomatoes, and stock; cover, and cook on Low for 6 to 8 hours.

3. Just before serving, stir in the peas and coconut milk and season with salt. Taste to adjust the seasonings.

South African Slow-Cooked Bobotie

This curry-flavored casserole is reminiscent of the South African favorite and is well suited to the slow cooker. Almond butter is available in well-stocked supermarkets and health food stores.

Slow Cooker Size:
3½ to 4 quart

Cook Time: 4 to 6 hours

Setting: Low

Serves 4

---

2 tablespoons olive oil
1 large yellow onion, chopped
1 tablespoon curry powder
1 pound vegetarian burger crumbles
4 cups diced fresh bread cubes
8 dried apricots, soaked for 10 minutes in hot water, drained, and chopped
Salt and freshly ground black pepper
1½ cups vegetable stock (see A Note About Stock, page 32)
⅓ cup apricot jam
⅓ cup almond butter
1 tablespoon fresh lemon juice
¼ cup sliced almonds, toasted (page 185)

1. Heat the oil in a large skillet over medium heat. Add the onion, cover, and cook until softened, about 5 minutes. Add the curry powder, stirring to coat.

2. Transfer the onion mixture to a 3½- to 4-quart slow cooker. Add the burger crumbles, bread cubes, and apricots, season with salt and pepper, and stir to combine.

3. In a blender or food processor, combine the stock, jam, almond butter, and lemon juice and process well. Pour the mixture into the slow cooker, stirring to combine. Cover and cook on Low for 4 to 6 hours.

4. Sprinkle with the almonds and serve.

Slow-Fashioned Potpie with Biscuit Crust

The steam heat produces a soft and tender biscuit crust. If you prefer a drier crust, let the cooked potpie sit uncovered for 5 to 10 minutes before serving. This quick and easy method for the crust is similar to drop biscuits. For a smooth, more uniform crust, roll out the dough on a lightly floured surface to a $1/4$-inch-thick circle and carefully place it on top of the cooking vegetables.

Slow Cooker Size:
$3\frac{1}{2}$ to 4 quart

Cook Time: 6 hours

Setting: 5 hours on Low; 1 hour on High

Serves 4

3 tablespoons olive oil

1 medium-size yellow onion, chopped

1 large carrot, chopped

1 cup plus 2 tablespoons all-purpose flour

1 large all-purpose potato, peeled and diced

3 cups slow-cooked (page 95) or two 15.5-ounces can chickpeas, drained and rinsed

$\frac{1}{2}$ cup frozen peas

$\frac{3}{4}$ cup vegetable stock (see A Note About Stock, page 32)

1 tablespoon tamari or other soy sauce

$\frac{1}{2}$ teaspoon dried thyme

$\frac{1}{2}$ teaspoon dried savory

Salt and freshly ground black pepper

2 teaspoons baking powder

$\frac{1}{2}$ teaspoon baking soda

$\frac{1}{2}$ cup milk or soy milk

1. Heat 1 tablespoon of the oil in a medium-size skillet over medium heat. Add the onion and carrot, cover, and cook until softened, about 5 minutes.

2. Transfer the onion and carrot to a lightly oiled $3\frac{1}{2}$- to 4-quart slow cooker. Stir in 2 tablespoons of the flour. Add the potato, chickpeas, and peas, stir in the stock, tamari, thyme, and savory, and season with salt and pepper. Cover and cook on Low for 5 hours.

3. About 1 hour before you're ready to serve, make the crust: In a large bowl, combine the remaining 1 cup flour, the baking powder, baking soda, and $\frac{1}{2}$ teaspoon salt. Quickly stir in the milk and the remaining 2 tablespoons oil until just blended.

4. Spoon the biscuit topping over the surface of the simmering vegetables. Turn the heat setting to High, cover, and cook until the crust is cooked through, about 1 hour longer. Serve the potpie within 10 to 15 minutes after the crust is finished cooking for best taste results.

Cornbread-Topped Southwestern Potpie

The steamy heat of the slow cooker allows the cornbread to cook right on top of the simmering vegetables. For a more rustic topping, omit the step for rolling out the cornbread. Instead, simply spoon the cornbread mixture onto the vegetables and spread it over the top.

Slow Cooker Size:
3½ to 4 quart

Cook Time: 6 hours

Setting: 5 hours on Low; 1 hour on High

Serves 4

3 tablespoons olive oil
1 small yellow onion, chopped
1 medium-size carrot, chopped
½ small red bell pepper, seeded and chopped
2 garlic cloves, minced
1 cup frozen corn kernels
3 cups slow-cooked (page 95) or two 15.5-ounce cans pinto beans, drained and rinsed
One 4-ounce can chopped green chiles, drained
¾ cup vegetable stock (see A Note About Stock, page 32)
1 tablespoon tamari or other soy sauce
1 tablespoon minced fresh cilantro leaves
Salt and freshly ground black pepper
1 cup cornmeal
2 teaspoons baking powder
½ teaspoon baking soda
½ cup milk or soy milk

1. Heat 1 tablespoon of the oil in a skillet over medium heat. Add the onion and carrot, cover, and cook until softened, about 5 minutes.

2. Transfer the onion and carrot to a lightly oiled 3½- to 4-quart slow cooker and add the bell pepper, garlic, corn, pinto beans, and chiles. Stir in the stock, tamari, and cilantro, and season with salt and pepper. Cover and cook on Low for 5 hours.

3. About 1 hour before you're ready to serve, make the topping: In a large bowl, combine the cornmeal, baking powder, baking soda, and ½ teaspoon salt. Add the milk and the remaining 2 tablespoons oil and stir to blend.

4. On a lightly floured work surface, roll out the dough to a ¼-inch-thick circle, then carefully place the crust on top of the cooking vegetables. Turn the heat setting to High, cover, and cook until the topping is cooked through, about 1 hour longer. For best taste results, serve the potpie within 10 to 15 minutes after the crust is finished cooking.

Enchilada-Inspired Polenta Pie

The flavors and ingredients of enchiladas were the inspiration for this recipe, with a polenta base standing in for soft corn tortillas. For added richness, top with shredded cheddar or soy cheddar close to serving time.

Slow Cooker Size:
3½ to 4 quart

Cook Time: 6 to 8 hours
(bean topping added 30
minutes before serving)

Setting: Low

Serves 4

2 tablespoons olive oil
1 small yellow onion, minced
1¼ cups cornmeal
1 teaspoon salt
1 tablespoon plus ½ teaspoon chili powder
4 cups boiling water
2½ cups chunky salsa of your choice
1½ cups slow-cooked (page 95) or one 15.5-ounce cans pinto beans,
    drained and rinsed
1½ cups fresh or frozen corn kernels, thawed if necessary
One 4-ounce can diced green chiles, drained
2 tablespoons minced red onion
2 tablespoons sliced pitted black olives
Salt and freshly ground black pepper
2 tablespoons minced fresh cilantro leaves

1. Heat the oil in a small skillet over medium heat. Add the onion, cover, and cook until softened, about 5 minutes.

2. Transfer the onion to a lightly oiled 3½- to 4-quart slow cooker. Add the cornmeal, salt, and ½ teaspoon of the chili powder. Stir in the boiling water until well combined. Cover and cook on Low for 6 to 8 hours, stirring occasionally.

3. In a large bowl, combine the salsa, beans, corn, chiles, red onion, olives, and remaining 1 tablespoon chili powder and season with salt and pepper. Mix well and set aside.

4. About 30 minutes before ready to serve, spread the bean mixture over the top of the polenta. Cover and continue to cook on Low until the bean mixture is hot.

5. Serve garnished with the cilantro.

Seitan from Scratch

Seitan (wheat-meat) is best when left to gently simmer for several hours and, once again, the slow cooker comes to the rescue. For a firmer texture, add $^1/_4$ cup of powdered wheat gluten to the mix. The cooking liquid may be strained and used as a stock in sauces, soups, and other recipes. This recipe calls for a 6-quart slow cooker. To make it in a smaller cooker, cook the seitan in less water with fewer vegetables— just enough to make everything fit.

Slow Cooker Size:
6 quart

Cook Time: 4 to 6 hours
(plus 1 hour to heat
stock while preparing
the seitan)

Setting: 1 hour on High;
4 to 6 hours on Low

Makes about 2
pounds

1 large carrot, cut into 2-inch chunks
1 large yellow onion, quartered
3 garlic cloves, crushed
½ cup tamari or other soy sauce
2 bay leaves
2½ quarts plus 3 cups water, or more as needed
6 cups whole-wheat flour (about 2 pounds)

1. Combine the carrot, onion, garlic, tamari, and bay leaves in a 6-quart slow cooker. Add 2½ quarts of the water, cover, and turn the heat setting to High.

2. Place the flour in a large bowl and add the remaining 3 cups water. Stir well to combine, adding a little more water if the dough is too dry. Turn the dough out onto a flat surface and knead until it is smooth and elastic, about 10 minutes. Place the dough back in the bowl and add enough warm water to cover. Let it rest for 20 minutes.

3. Place the bowl holding the dough and water in the sink. Knead the dough in the bowl until the water turns white. Drain the liquid, then cover with fresh water and knead again until the water in the bowl turns white. Repeat the process, using fresh water each time, until the water is almost clear. The dough should now be a smooth ball of wheat gluten, or raw seitan.

4. Depending on how you plan to use it, leave the raw seitan whole or divide into 4 smaller pieces and add to the simmering stock. Change the heat setting to Low, cover, and cook for 4 to 6 hours.

5. Remove the cooked seitan from the cooker and transfer to a baking sheet to cool. If you are not using the seitan right away, it can be stored submerged in its stock in the refrigerator in a tightly covered container for up to 5 days or frozen for several weeks.

Not Your Mama's Pot Roast

Seitan Quick Mix (available in natural food stores) is used to make this vegetarian pot roast. If you can't find it, you can make your own seitan using the recipe for Seitan from Scratch on page 129. If you're short on time, buy a package of precooked seitan available in the refrigerator case of natural food stores and add the seitan chunks to the simmering vegetables. To make a gravy from the cooking liquid, remove the solid ingredients, turn the cooker to High, and whisk in one tablespoon of cornstarch blended with two tablespoons of water and stir until it thickens.

Slow Cooker Size:
5½ to 6 quart

Cook Time: 8 hours

Setting: Low

Serves 4

One 6-ounce box Seitan Quick Mix
½ teaspoon onion powder
½ teaspoon dried thyme
½ teaspoon salt
⅛ teaspoon freshly ground black pepper
½ cup water, or more as needed
3 tablespoons tamari or other soy sauce
1 tablespoon olive oil
2 small sweet yellow onions, halved or quartered
1 pound baby carrots
1 pound small new potatoes, halved
Salt and freshly ground black pepper
1½ cups vegetable stock (see A Note About Stock, page 32)
¼ cup dry red wine
2 garlic cloves, crushed
1 teaspoon dried thyme

1. In a large bowl, combine the seitan mix, onion powder, thyme, salt, and pepper. Add the water and 2 tablespoons of the tamari. Mix well, adding more water if the mixture is too dry, then knead until smooth, about 3 minutes. Place the seitan ball in 5½- to 6-quart slow cooker.

2. In a large skillet, heat the oil over medium-high heat. Add the onions, carrots, and potatoes and brown quickly. Season with salt and pepper, then transfer to the slow cooker. Add the stock, wine, the remaining 1 tablespoon tamari, the garlic, and thyme. Cover and cook on Low for 8 hours.

3. Remove the vegetables and seitan from the slow cooker. Slice the seitan and arrange on a serving platter. Surround with the vegetables and spoon the cooking liquid or gravy (see headnote) over all.

Braised Seitan with Red Wine and Mushrooms

The final step of thickening the luscious red wine sauce may be omitted if you prefer, but I think the added richness of the mushroom purée is worth the extra effort. Gravy Master, available in supermarkets, is a browning liquid containing no animal ingredients that deepens the color of the sauce to a luxurious brown. Serve over rice or wide noodles.

Slow Cooker Size:
3½ to 4 quart

Cook Time: 6 to 8 hours

Setting: Low

Serves 4

2 tablespoons olive oil
1 pound seitan, cut into ½-inch-thick slices
6 shallots, quartered
2 garlic cloves, minced
8 ounces small white mushrooms, sliced or quartered
½ cup vegetable stock (see A Note About Stock, page 95)
2 tablespoons tomato paste
½ cup dry red wine
1 tablespoon minced fresh thyme leaves or 1 teaspoon dried
Salt and freshly ground black pepper
½ teaspoon Gravy Master or other vegetarian browning liquid

1. Heat 1 tablespoon of the oil in a large skillet over medium heat. Add the seitan and cook until browned on all sides, about 10 minutes. Remove with a slotted spoon and set aside.

2. Reheat the skillet over medium heat with the remaining 1 table-spoon oil. Add the shallots and cook, stirring a few times, until softened and slightly browned, about 5 minutes. Stir in the garlic and cook until fragrant, about 30 seconds.

3. Place the shallot mixture in a 3½- to 4-quart slow cooker. Add the mushrooms and seitan. Stir in the stock, tomato paste, wine, and dried thyme, if using, and season with salt and pepper. Cover and cook on Low for 6 to 8 hours.

4. Near the end of cooking time, stir in the fresh thyme, if using. When ready to serve, scoop out about 1 cup of the mushrooms with a small amount of the liquid and pour into a blender or food processor. Add the Gravy Master and process until smooth, then stir back into the cooker to thicken the sauce.

Barbecued Seitan and Layered Vegetables

Sweet and sticky barbecue sauce permeates the layers of vegetables and seitan for a wholesome, down-home meal. Since the peels are the most nutritious part of the potato, I like to leave them on whenever possible, such as in this recipe. Just be sure to scrub them well before using.

Slow Cooker Size:
4 quart

Cook Time: 6 to 8 hours

Setting: Low

Serves 4

---

2 tablespoons olive oil

1 large yellow onion, cut in half and thinly sliced into half moons

2 large Yukon Gold potatoes, cut into ¼-inch-thick slices

1 large red or yellow bell pepper, seeded and thinly sliced into rings

1 large carrot, shredded

1 medium-size zucchini, thinly sliced

12 ounces seitan, cut into ¼-inch-thick slices

One 6-ounce can tomato paste

1 teaspoon dry mustard

¼ cup dark unsulfured molasses

¼ cup tamari or other soy sauce

2 tablespoons cider vinegar

2 tablespoons packed light brown sugar

1 cup water

1. Heat 1 tablespoon of the oil in a skillet over medium-high heat. Add the onion and cook, stirring, until slightly browned, about 5 minutes. Transfer to a 4-quart slow cooker. Add the potatoes to the same skillet, cook until browned, and arrange on top of the onions in the cooker. On top of the onions and potato slices, layer the bell pepper, carrot, and zucchini.

2. Heat the remaining 1 tablespoon oil in the same skillet over medium-high heat. Add the seitan and cook until browned on both sides, 7 to 10 minutes. Layer it over the top of the vegetables in the slow cooker.

3. In a small bowl, combine the tomato paste, mustard, molasses, tamari, vinegar, brown sugar, and water and pour over the ingredients in the slow cooker. Cover and cook on Low for 6 to 8 hours.

Slow-Cooked Tomato Sauce for Pasta

Serve this sauce over your favorite freshly cooked pasta. This sauce can be cooled, portioned into tightly sealed containers, and stored in the refrigerator or freezer for future use. Refrigerated, it will keep for several days; frozen, it will keep well for up to one month.

Slow Cooker Size:
4 quart

Cook Time: 6 hours

Setting: Low

Makes about 3 quarts

2 tablespoons olive oil
1 large yellow onion, chopped
1 small red bell pepper, seeded and chopped
1 medium-size carrot, finely shredded
2 garlic cloves, minced
Three 28-ounce cans crushed tomatoes
½ cup dry red wine
1 to 2 teaspoons packed light brown sugar, to your taste
2 teaspoons dried basil
1 teaspoon dried oregano
1 teaspoon salt
¼ teaspoon freshly ground black pepper

1. Heat the oil in a medium-size skillet over medium heat. Add the onion, bell pepper, carrot, and garlic, cover, and cook until softened, about 5 minutes.

2. Transfer the vegetable mixture to a 4-quart slow cooker. Add the tomatoes, wine, brown sugar, basil, oregano, salt, and pepper. Cover, and cook on Low for 6 hours.

Fettuccine with Lentil Bolognese Sauce

In Bologna, tagliatelle is the pasta of choice for their famous meat sauce, but I like to use nontraditional fettuccine to go with this nontraditional version of the sauce.

Slow Cooker Size:
3½ to 4 quart

Cook Time: 6 hours

Setting: Low

Serves 4

2 tablespoons olive oil
1 small yellow onion, minced
1 small carrot, minced
1 celery rib, minced
2 garlic cloves, minced
½ cup dry white wine
One 28-ounce can crushed tomatoes
1 cup dried brown lentils, picked over and rinsed
2 tablespoons tomato paste dissolved in 1 cup hot water
Pinch of ground nutmeg
Salt and freshly ground black pepper
½ cup slow-cooked (page 95) or canned white beans, drained and rinsed
¼ cup milk or soy milk
1 pound fettuccine
½ teaspoon Liquid Smoke
2 tablespoons minced fresh Italian parsley leaves
Freshly grated Parmesan cheese or soy Parmesan to serve

1. Heat the oil in a large skillet over medium heat. Add the onion, carrot, celery, and garlic, cover, and cook until softened, about 10 minutes. Stir in the wine and simmer for 2 minutes.

2. Transfer the vegetable mixture to a 3½- to 4-quart slow cooker. Add the tomatoes, lentils, tomato paste mixture, and nutmeg and season with salt and pepper. Cover and cook on Low for 6 hours.

3. While the lentil sauce is cooking, combine the beans and milk in a blender or food processor and blend until smooth. Set aside.

4. When ready to serve, cook the pasta in a large pot of boiling salted water, stirring occasionally, until it is *al dente*, about 8 minutes. Drain well.

5. Just prior to serving, stir the bean mixture, Liquid Smoke, and parsley into the sauce. Place the cooked pasta in a serving bowl, add the sauce, toss gently to combine, and serve immediately with the cheese.

Slow-Cooked Ziti Casserole

Slow cooking is a great way to enjoy a comforting casserole without heating up the kitchen. In this recipe, cooked pasta is added during the final 20 to 30 minutes before serving. As an alternative, you can add uncooked pasta at the beginning of the cooking time along with an extra cup of water, although the pasta may turn out starchy.

Slow Cooker Size:
4 quart

Cook Time: 4 hours
(pasta is added during the last 20 to 30 minutes)

Setting: Low

Serves 4

2 tablespoons olive oil
1 large onion, minced
2 garlic cloves, minced
One 28-ounce can crushed tomatoes
One 12-ounce package frozen vegetarian burger crumbles
1 cup hot water
½ cup dry red wine
1 tablespoon chopped fresh basil leaves or 1 teaspoon dried
Salt and freshly ground black pepper
8 ounces ziti, cooked according to package instructions until *al dente*, drained, and rinsed
2 tablespoons chopped fresh parsley leaves
⅓ cup freshly grated Parmesan or soy Parmesan cheese

1. Heat the oil in a large skillet over medium heat, add the onion, cover, and cook until softened, about 5 minutes. Add the garlic and cook until fragrant, about 30 seconds.

2. Transfer the onion mixture to a 4-quart slow cooker. Add the tomatoes, burger crumbles, hot water, wine, and dried basil if using, and season with salt and pepper. Cover and cook on Low for 3½ hours.

3. Stir in the ziti, cover, and cook on Low for another 20 to 30 minutes to heat through.

4. When ready to serve, stir in the parsley and fresh basil, if using, and sprinkle with the cheese.

Vegetable Lasagna

Slow-cooked lasagna may sound unconventional, but it tastes great and is convenient to make. You will need to break the lasagna noodles to conform to the shape of the slow cooker. If you use a large, shallow cooker, it will more closely resemble a typical lasagna casserole.

Slow Cooker Size:
4 to 6 quart

Cook Time: 4 hours

Setting: Low

Serves 6

2 tablespoons olive oil
1 small yellow onion, minced
1 large zucchini, shredded
8 ounces white mushrooms, sliced
2 garlic cloves, minced
½ teaspoon dried basil
½ teaspoon dried oregano
Salt and freshly ground black pepper
1 roasted red bell pepper, chopped (see Note)
1 pound firm tofu, drained
1 pound soft tofu, drained
⅓ cup freshly grated Parmesan cheese or soy Parmesan
¼ cup minced fresh parsley leaves
3 cups seasoned tomato sauce, bottled or homemade (page 133)
8 ounces no-boil lasagna noodles
1½ cups shredded mozzarella or soy mozzarella cheese

1. Heat the oil in a medium-size skillet over medium heat. Add the onion, cover, and cook until softened, about 5 minutes. Add the zucchini, mushrooms, garlic, basil, and oregano, season with salt and pepper, and cook until the vegetables soften, about 5 minutes. Stir in the roasted bell pepper and set aside.

2. In a large bowl with a wooden spoon, combine both tofus, the Parmesan, and parsley until well mixed; season with salt and pepper. Add the sautéed vegetable mixture and stir to combine well.

3. Spread a thin layer of tomato sauce over the bottom of a 4- to 6-quart slow cooker. Top with a layer of noodles. Top the noodles with half of the tofu-vegetable mixture, followed by another layer of noodles. Spread a layer of sauce over the noodles and sprinkle with one quarter of the mozzarella. Repeat the layering until the ingredients are used up, ending with a layer of tomato sauce topped with the remaining shredded cheese. Cover and cook on Low for 4 hours.

4. Remove the lid and let stand at room temperature for 15 minutes before serving.

Note: Roasted red bell peppers, packed in oil and sold in jars, are widely available in supermarkets. To roast your own using a fresh bell pepper, hold it over a flame until the skin turns black and blisters, then place inside a paper or plastic bag for several minutes. Remove from the bag, scrape off the blackened part, and remove the stem, seeds, and membrane. Proceed with recipe.

Mac and Cheese Florentine

This yummy comfort-food casserole is so rich and flavorful, it's hard to believe it's good for you. The creamy sauce is made with puréed white beans and cashews, resulting in loads of protein and flavor without a speck of dairy. The addition of spinach makes it an easy one-dish meal that is especially suited to lazy summer suppers when you might enjoy a comforting casserole but don't want to turn on the oven.

Slow Cooker Size:
4 quart

Cook Time: 3 hours

Setting: Low

Serves 4

---

8 ounces elbow macaroni

One 10-ounce package frozen chopped spinach, cooked according to package instructions and well drained

2 tablespoons olive oil

1 medium-size yellow onion, chopped

½ cup unsalted raw cashews

1¾ cups water

1½ cups slow-cooked (page 95) or one 15.5-ounce can white beans, drained and rinsed

1 tablespoon white miso paste (optional)

2 teaspoons fresh lemon juice

¼ teaspoon dry mustard

¼ teaspoon cayenne pepper

Pinch of ground nutmeg

Salt

½ cup dry bread crumbs

1. Cook the macaroni in a pot of salted boiling water until *al dente*, about 8 minutes. Drain and place in a large bowl. Add the spinach and toss to combine. Set aside.

2. Heat 1 tablespoon of the oil in a medium-size skillet over medium heat, add the onion, cover, and cook until softened, about 5 minutes. Set aside.

3. Grind the cashews to a powder in a blender or food processor. Add 1 cup of the water and blend until smooth. Add the onion, beans, miso paste, if using, the remaining ¾ cup water, the lemon juice, mustard, cayenne, and nutmeg and season with salt. (The amount of salt you need depends on whether or not you use the miso paste, which tends to be salty.) Blend until smooth, then taste to adjust the seasonings. Pour the sauce over the macaroni and spinach and mix well.

4. Transfer the mixture to a lightly oiled 4-quart slow cooker. Cover and cook on Low for 3 hours.

5. Close to serving time, heat the remaining 1 tablespoon oil in a small skillet over medium heat. Add the bread crumbs, stirring to coat them with the oil. Cook, stirring, until lightly toasted, 3 to 4 minutes. Remove from the heat and set aside. When ready to serve, sprinkle the toasted crumbs on top of the casserole.

Black-Eyed Peas and Chard with Soba Noodles

The robust character of soba, Japanese buckwheat noodles, complements the hearty flavor of the black-eyed peas. Some varieties of chard have thick tough stems, while other varieties are more leafy with tender stems. If using thick-stemmed chard, cut the stems away from the leaves so you can cook the stems a little longer than the rest of the chard.

Slow Cooker Size:
3½ to 4 quart

Cook Time: 6 to 8 hours

Setting: Low

Serves 4

1 bunch Swiss chard, washed and leaves cut away from thick stems
2 tablespoons olive oil
1 large carrot, halved lengthwise and cut on a diagonal into ¼-inch-thick slices
2 shallots, minced
2 garlic cloves, minced
3 cups slow-cooked (page 95) or two 15.5-ounce cans black-eyed peas, drained and rinsed
1 cup vegetable stock (see A Note About Stock, page 32)
Salt and freshly ground black pepper
One 8-ounce package soba noodles

1. If using thick chard stems, cut them into ¼-inch slices and cook in a pot of boiling salted water for 5 minutes. Cut the chard leaves into ½-inch-wide strips and add to the same pot of water until tender, about 3 to 4 minutes longer. Drain and set aside.

2. Heat the oil in a medium-size skillet over medium heat. Add the carrot, shallots, and garlic, cover, and cook until softened, about 5 minutes.

3. Transfer the carrot mixture to a 3½- to 4-quart slow cooker. Add the black-eyed peas and stock, season with salt and pepper, cover, and cook on Low for 6 to 8 hours.

4. Stir in the chard and taste to adjust the seasonings.

5. When ready to serve, cook the soba according to package directions. Drain well and place in a large bowl. Top with the pea-and-chard mixture and serve at once.

The Stuffing
and the Stuffed

• • •

The next time you're in the mood for stuffed vege-
tables—from bell peppers to zucchini—get out your slow cooker and
start stuffing. The slow cooker is an ideal way to cook stuffed
vegetables because its gentle, continuous heat surrounds the
vegetables, making them tender and delicious without
the drying or scorching that can sometimes happen in
the oven.

This chapter is loaded with variations to add to your
stuffed vegetable repertoire, from Bell Peppers Stuffed
with Salsa Rice and Beans (page 151) to Bulgur and
Lentil Stuffed Eggplant (page 158). And the combina-
tions are increased because you can mix-and-match the
various stuffings with the vegetable of your choice.
For example, you can use the Salsa Rice and Beans
(page 151) to stuff squash instead of bell peppers. Because of
their size, most stuffed vegetables need to be cooked in a 5½- to 6-quart

slow cooker. If all you have is a smaller cooker, then, in most cases, you will need to cut the recipe in half.

Slow cookers are also great for cooking stuffing on its own—especially those wonderful savory bread stuffings often associated with holiday meals. The stuffing recipes in this chapter, such as Wild Mushroom Stuffing (page 144) and Chestnut and Apple Stuffing (page 146), are so rich and flavorful, they can be served as a main course.

For a heartier entrée option, try the Savory Stuffed Wheat Meat Roast (page 166)—chewy and flavorful seitan wrapped around a delicious bread stuffing. As a special nod to my husband's Scottish heritage, I've also included an unusual recipe for vegetarian haggis—a flavorful oat-and-vegetable stuffing that can be cooked in a sheet of bean curd skin or enjoyed on its own or as a stuffing for vegetables.

From casual weeknight suppers to holiday feasts, this chapter has recipes everyone can enjoy.

Troubleshooting Tips for Slow-Cooked Stuffing

Stuffing can sometimes toughen and harden at the edges when overcooked or cooked at a temperature that is too high. To avoid this you should always:

- Cook no longer than three hours
- Cook on Low

Other solutions include:

- Stir occasionally
- Place your stuffing in a covered casserole dish to cook inside the slow cooker (set it on a rack or trivet with an inch of water on the bottom of the cooker).

Wild Mushroom Stuffing

Three kinds of mushrooms, both dried and fresh, provide intense mushroom flavor in this stuffing. If serving it as a main course, you can boost the protein by adding up to two cups of cooked and crumbled soy sausage. Be sure to cook this and other bread stuffing recipes on Low because the edges tend to become overcooked on High.

Slow Cooker Size:
4 quart

Cook Time: 3 to 4 hours

Setting: Low

Serves 8

¼ cup dried porcini mushrooms

1 cup boiling water

2 tablespoons olive oil

1 medium-size yellow onion, chopped

1 celery rib, chopped

4 ounces cremini mushrooms, coarsely chopped

4 ounces oyster mushrooms, coarsely chopped

1 teaspoon dried thyme

1 teaspoon ground sage

8 cups ½-inch bread cubes

2 tablespoons minced fresh parsley leaves

1 teaspoon salt

¼ teaspoon freshly ground black pepper

1 to 1½ cups vegetable stock (see A Note About Stock, page 32), as needed

1. Soak the dried porcini in the boiling water for 30 minutes. Drain, reserving ½ cup of the soaking liquid. Rinse the mushrooms, then chop them.

2. Heat the oil in a large skillet over medium heat. Add the onion and celery, cover, and cook until softened, about 5 minutes. Add all the mushrooms, the thyme, and sage, stirring to coat.

3. Transfer the cooked vegetables to a 4-quart slow cooker and add the bread cubes, parsley, salt, and pepper. Stir in the reserved mushroom soaking liquid and just enough stock to moisten, then smooth the top, cover, and cook on Low for 3 to 4 hours. Serve hot.

Cranberry-Walnut Stuffing

This stuffing is a symphony of textures and flavors thanks to the addition of crunchy walnuts, sweet-tart cranberries, and a splash of brandy.

Slow Cooker Size:
4 quart

Cook Time: 3 to 4 hours

Setting: Low

Serves 8

2 tablespoons olive oil
1 medium-size yellow onion, chopped
1 celery rib, chopped
1 teaspoon dried thyme
1 teaspoon ground sage
2 tablespoons brandy
8 cups ½-inch bread cubes
1 cup chopped walnuts
⅓ cup sweetened dried cranberries
¼ cup minced fresh parsley leaves
1 teaspoon salt
¼ teaspoon freshly ground black pepper
1½ to 2 cups vegetable stock (see A Note About Stock page 32), as needed

1. Heat the oil in a large skillet over medium heat. Add the onion and celery, cover, and cook until softened, about 5 minutes. Add the thyme and sage, stirring to coat. Stir in the brandy and cook for 1 minute.

2. Transfer the mixture to a 4-quart slow cooker. Add the bread cubes, walnuts, cranberries, parsley, salt, and pepper; stir in just enough stock to moisten, and mix well. Taste and adjust the seasonings, adding a little more stock if the mixture is too dry. Cover and cook on Low for 3 to 4 hours. Serve hot.

Chestnut and Apple Stuffing

Canned or bottled chestnuts come ready to use and are available at well-stocked supermarkets and gourmet shops. Although fresh chestnuts are more economical, they are time-consuming to prepare. The choice is yours, but if you're interested in using fresh ones, see Preparing Fresh Chestnuts, below.

Slow Cooker Size:
4 to 6 quart

Cook Time: 3 to 4 hours

Setting: Low

Serves 8

2 tablespoons olive oil
1 large yellow onion, chopped
1 celery rib, chopped
1 teaspoon ground sage
½ teaspoon dried thyme
1 cup coarsely chopped cooked chestnuts
2 Granny Smith apples, peeled, cored, and chopped
8 cups ½-inch bread cubes
3 tablespoons minced fresh parsley leaves
1 teaspoon salt
¼ teaspoon freshly ground black pepper
1 to 1½ cups vegetable stock (see A Note About Stock, page 32), as needed

Preparing Fresh Chestnuts

Pierce the flat side of the shells with a sharp knife and make an "X." Boil the chestnuts or roast them at 350°F until the shells curl back. Remove the outer shell and inner skin with a sharp paring knife while the chestnuts are still hot for easier peeling.

1. Heat the oil in a large skillet over medium heat. Add the onion and celery, cover, and cook until softened, about 5 minutes. Stir in the sage and thyme.

2. Transfer the mixture to a 4- to 6-quart slow cooker and add the chestnuts, apples, bread cubes, parsley, salt, and pepper. Stir in just enough stock to moisten and mix well to combine. Taste to adjust the seasonings, cover, and cook on Low for 3 to 4 hours. Serve hot.

Wild Rice and Dried Fruit Stuffing

Wild rice and plumped bits of dried fruit are featured in this elegant and easy stuffing.

Slow Cooker Size:
4 to 6 quart

Cook Time: 5 hours

Setting: 3 hours on
High; 2 hours on Low

Serves 6 to 8

2 tablespoons olive oil
1 large yellow onion, chopped
2 celery ribs, chopped
½ cup wild rice
2¾ cups vegetable stock (see A Note About Stock, page 32)
Salt and freshly ground black pepper
1 cup mixed dried fruit, chopped, such as raisins, dried apricots,
   dried apple
Boiling water as needed
6 cups ½-inch bread cubes
¼ cup minced fresh parsley leaves
1 teaspoon dried thyme

1. Heat the oil in a large skillet over medium heat. Add the onion and celery, cover, and cook until softened, about 5 minutes.

2. Transfer the onion mixture to a 4- to 6-quart slow cooker. Add the rice and stock, season with salt and pepper to taste, and stir to combine. Cover and cook on Low until the rice is tender, about 3 hours.

3. Meanwhile, place the dried fruit in a small heatproof bowl. Cover with boiling water to soften for 15 minutes. Drain and set aside.

4. Once the rice is tender, stir in the bread cubes, parsley, thyme, and the softened fruit. Taste to adjust the seasonings. Change the heat setting to Low, cover, and cook for another 2 hours. Serve hot.

Old-Fashioned Bread Stuffing

This is a basic bread stuffing with no bells and whistles—just old-fashioned goodness like Mom used to make, with the added convenience of a slow cooker.

Slow Cooker Size:
4 quart

Cook Time: 3 to 4 hours

Setting: Low

Serves 8

2 tablespoons olive oil
1 large yellow onion, chopped
2 celery ribs, chopped
1 teaspoon ground sage
1 teaspoon dried marjoram
1 teaspoon dried thyme
10 cups ½-inch bread cubes
¼ cup minced fresh parsley leaves
1 teaspoon salt
¼ teaspoon freshly ground black pepper
1 to 1½ cups vegetable stock (see A Note About Stock, page 32), as needed

1. Heat the oil in a large skillet over medium heat. Add the onion and celery, cover, and cook until softened, about 5 minutes. Stir in the sage, marjoram, and thyme.

2. Place the bread cubes in a 4-quart slow cooker and add the parsley, salt, pepper, and onion mixture. Stir in just enough stock to moisten. Cover and cook on Low for 3 to 4 hours. Serve hot.

Spicy Basque Stuffing

This flavorful stuffing is adapted from my friend Lisa's family recipe, which uses tofu to replace the traditional chorizo sausage. I occasionally use crumbled soy sausage instead of the tofu with delicious results.

Slow Cooker Size:
4 to 6 quart

Cook Time: 3 to 4 hours

Setting: Low

Serves 6 to 8

2 tablespoons olive oil

1 large yellow onion, chopped

1 small green bell pepper, seeded and chopped

1 celery rib, chopped

2 garlic cloves, chopped

6 cups ½-inch bread cubes

1 pound firm tofu, drained and crumbled

2 tablespoons tamari or other soy sauce

2 cooking apples, like Granny Smith or McIntosh, peeled, cored, and chopped

3 tablespoons chopped fresh parsley leaves

1 teaspoon sugar or a natural sweetener

1 teaspoon salt

1 teaspoon dried thyme

½ teaspoon red pepper flakes

½ teaspoon ground sage

¼ teaspoon ground cumin

¼ teaspoon turmeric

¼ teaspoon cayenne pepper

¼ teaspoon ground cloves

¼ teaspoon ground nutmeg

¼ teaspoon freshly ground black pepper

1. Heat the oil in a large skillet over medium heat. Add the onion, bell pepper, celery, and garlic, cover, and cook until softened, about 10 minutes.

2. Combine the bread cubes, tofu, tamari, apples, parsley, sugar, salt, spices, and onion mixture in a 4- to 6-quart slow cooker. Stir well to combine, adding just enough water to moisten. Taste to adjust the seasonings, cover, and cook on Low for 3 to 4 hours. Serve hot.

Savory Vegetable Bread Pudding

This versatile bread pudding can be enjoyed for brunch, lunch, or dinner. It can be assembled in advance and refrigerated right in the slow cooker insert.

Slow Cooker Size:
4 to 6 quart

Cook Time: 4 to 5 hours

Setting: Low

Serves 6 to 8

2 tablespoons olive oil
1 medium-size yellow onion, chopped
½ small red bell pepper, seeded and chopped
1 medium-size carrot, shredded
1 small zucchini, shredded
4 ounces white mushrooms, sliced
2 garlic cloves, minced
Salt and freshly ground black pepper
1½ cups slow-cooked (page 95) or one 15.5-ounce can navy or other white beans, drained and rinsed
2 cups vegetable stock (see A Note About Stock, page 32)
1½ teaspoons Dijon mustard
1 teaspoon minced fresh savory leaves or ¼ teaspoon dried
¾ teaspoon salt
⅛ teaspoon cayenne pepper
4 ounces mozzarella cheese or soy mozzarella, shredded
1 loaf Italian bread, sliced

1. Heat the oil in a large skillet over medium heat. Add the onion, cover, and cook until softened, about 5 minutes. Add the bell pepper, carrot, zucchini, mushrooms, and garlic; season with salt and pepper to taste, and cook until slightly softened, about 3 minutes. Remove from the heat.

2. In a food processor or blender, combine the beans, stock, mustard, savory, salt, and cayenne and process until smooth. Stir into the sautéed vegetables, then stir in the cheese.

3. Cut the bread slices into small pieces and arrange about one-third of the loaf in the bottom of a 4- to 6-quart slow cooker. Pour about one-third of the vegetable mixture over the bread, using a fork to distribute the vegetables evenly. Repeat with a second layer of bread, followed by a second layer of the vegetable mixture. Top with the remaining bread, pressing down gently to eliminate air pockets. Pour on the remaining vegetable mixture, spreading it evenly over the top layer of bread. Cover and cook on Low for 4 to 5 hours.

Bell Peppers Stuffed with Salsa Rice and Beans

Use red, green, or yellow bell peppers and hot or mild salsa, according to your preference.

Slow Cooker Size:
5½ to 6 quart

Cook Time: 4 hours

Setting: Low

Serves 4

4 large bell peppers
2½ cups cooked white or brown rice
1½ cups slow-cooked (page 95) or one 15.5-ounce can red kidney beans, drained and rinsed
1 cup tomato salsa
3 scallions, chopped
Salt and freshly ground black pepper
One 14.5-ounce can crushed tomatoes
½ teaspoon ground cumin
¼ teaspoon dried oregano
½ teaspoon sugar

1. Cut the tops off the bell peppers, save them for later use, and remove and discard the seeds and membranes. Arrange the peppers upright in a 5½- to 6-quart slow cooker.

2. In a medium-size mixing bowl, combine the rice, beans, salsa, and scallions and season with salt and pepper to taste. Mix well. Fill the pepper cavities evenly with the rice mixture, packing it lightly. Replace the pepper tops.

3. In the same bowl, combine the tomatoes, cumin, oregano, and sugar and season with salt and pepper to taste. Pour over and around the peppers in the slow cooker. Cover and cook on Low for 4 hours, until the peppers are fork-tender but still hold their shape. Serve hot.

Bell Peppers Stuffed with Israeli Couscous and Lentils

Israeli couscous, larger than regular couscous, combines well with lentils as the stuffing for bell peppers. The stuffing is also delicious on its own.

Slow Cooker Size:
5½ to 6 quart

Cook Time: 4 hours

Setting: Low

Serves 4

4 large red bell peppers
3 tablespoons olive oil
1 small yellow onion, minced
2 cups cooked Israeli couscous
1½ cups cooked lentils, drained
⅓ cup reconstituted or oil-packed sun-dried tomatoes, drained and chopped
1 tablespoon minced fresh parsley leaves
¼ teaspoon dried oregano
Salt and freshly ground black pepper
⅓ cup tomato paste
2 tablespoons orange juice
1 teaspoon sugar
½ teaspoon Dijon mustard
1 cup water
¼ teaspoon cayenne pepper (optional)

1. Slice off the tops of the peppers and remove and discard the seeds and membranes. Removing the stems, chop the pepper tops and set aside. Arrange the peppers upright in a 5½- to 6-quart slow cooker.

2. Heat 1 tablespoon of the oil in a large skillet over medium heat. Add the onion and chopped pepper tops, cover, and cook until softened, about 5 minutes.

3. In a medium-size mixing bowl, combine the couscous, lentils, onion mixture, sun-dried tomatoes, parsley, and oregano and season with salt and black pepper to taste. Mix well and spoon into the pepper cavities, packing lightly.

4. In the same bowl, combine the tomato paste, orange juice, sugar, mustard, and water, stirring to blend. Add the cayenne, if using, and season with salt and black pepper to taste. Pour over and around the peppers in the slow cooker. Cover and cook on Low for 4 hours, until the peppers are fork-tender but still hold their shape. Serve hot.

Bell Peppers Stuffed with Coconut Rice and Mangoes

The flavors of Thailand are the inspiration for this fresh take on stuffed peppers. The size of the peppers you use will determine the size of slow cooker required. You will need a 5½- to 6-quart cooker to fit four (or more) large peppers. If a smaller cooker is all you have, use smaller (or fewer) peppers.

Slow Cooker Size:
5½ to 6 quart

Cook Time: 4 hours

Setting: Low

Serves 4

4 large green or red bell peppers
2 tablespoons peanut oil
1 large red onion, chopped
2 cups cooked jasmine or other long-grain rice
½ cup unsweetened shredded coconut
½ cup chopped unsalted dry-roasted cashews or peanuts
½ cup chopped fresh Thai basil or cilantro leaves
2 teaspoons fresh lime juice
1 teaspoon sugar
Salt and freshly ground black pepper
1 ripe mango, peeled, halved, and halves cut away from the seed

1. Slice off the tops of the peppers and remove and discard the seeds and membranes. Removing the stems, chop the pepper tops and set aside. Arrange the peppers upright in a 5½- to 6-quart slow cooker.

2. Heat 1 tablespoon of the oil in a large skillet over medium heat. Add the onion and chopped pepper tops, cover, and cook until softened, about 5 minutes.

3. In a medium-size mixing bowl, combine the onion mixture, rice, coconut, cashews, basil, lime juice, and sugar and season with salt and pepper to taste. Chop one half of the mango and add to the stuffing. Mix well and spoon into the pepper cavities, packing it lightly. Cover and cook on Low for 4 hours, until the peppers are tender but still hold their shape.

4. Cut the remaining mango half into thin slices and use to garnish the peppers when ready to serve.

Golden-Glow Stuffed Squash

Use a dense, orange-fleshed squash, such as butternut, buttercup, kabocha, or acorn. A six-quart oval slow cooker works best in order to fit the squash halves inside. Otherwise, choose a squash that fits in your cooker whole and slice off the top few inches so you can scoop out the seeds and stuff it whole.

Slow Cooker Size:
6 quart oval

Cook Time: 6 hours

Setting: Low

Serves 4

1 tablespoon olive oil
1 medium-size yellow onion, minced
1 medium-size carrot, coarsely shredded
1 small yellow bell pepper, seeded and chopped
2 cloves garlic, minced
¼ teaspoon turmeric
2½ cups cooked white or brown rice
1 tablespoon minced fresh parsley leaves
1 teaspoon dried thyme or ground sage
Salt and freshly ground black pepper
1 large winter squash, halved and seeded
1 cup hot water

1. Heat the oil in a large skillet over medium heat. Add the onion, carrot, and bell pepper, cover, and cook until softened, about 5 minutes. Stir in the garlic and turmeric, then stir in the rice, parsley, and thyme and season with salt and pepper to taste. Mix well and spoon the mixture into the squash cavities.

2. Pour the water into a 6-quart oval slow cooker and add the squash halves, stuffing side up. Cover and cook on Low until the squash is tender, about 6 hours. Serve hot.

Winter Squash Stuffed with Couscous, Apricots, and Pistachios

This nourishing main dish tastes more like dessert to me, with its juice-sweetened spiced couscous and bits of apricot and pistachios. If you start with a really sweet squash such as kabocha, it's even better. To make cutting the squash easier, place it in the microwave for a minute or so, then let it sit another minute. Also, if your squash is lopsided, cut a sliver from the bottom and it will sit perfectly in the cooker.

Slow Cooker Size:
5½ to 6 quart

Cook Time: 6 hours

Setting: Low

Serves 4

2 cups apple juice
1 cup couscous
¼ teaspoon ground cinnamon
¼ teaspoon ground allspice
1 cup chopped dried apricots
2 tablespoons olive oil
1 large yellow onion, chopped
1 garlic clove, minced
½ cup chopped pistachio nuts
Salt and freshly ground black pepper
1 large kabocha, buttercup, or other winter squash, halved and seeded
1 cup hot water

1. Bring the apple juice to a boil in a medium-size saucepan. Add the couscous, cinnamon, and allspice. Reduce the heat to low, cover, and simmer for 10 minutes. Remove from the heat, stir in the apricots, cover, and set aside.

2. Heat the oil in a large skillet over medium heat. Add the onion and garlic, cover, and cook until softened, about 5 minutes.

3. Fluff the couscous with a fork, then add the onion mixture and pistachios, season with salt and pepper to taste, and mix well.

4. Place the squash halves, cut side up, in a 5½- to 6-quart slow cooker. Pack the stuffing into the squash halves. Carefully pour the hot water into the cooker without disturbing the squash. Cover and cook on Low until the squash is tender, about 6 hours. Serve hot.

Zucchini Stuffed with Tomato, White Beans, and Pesto

As with most stuffed vegetable recipes, this one will need a large cooker (preferably oval-shaped) in order to accommodate the shape of the zucchini.

Slow Cooker Size:
5½ to 6 quart oval

Cook Time: 3 to 4 hours

Setting: Low

Serves 4

2 large or 4 small zucchini, halved lengthwise and ends trimmed
2 tablespoons olive oil
2 shallots, minced
1 large garlic clove, minced
Salt and freshly ground black pepper
1 large ripe tomato, chopped
1½ cups slow-cooked (page 95) or one 15.5-ounce can white beans, drained and rinsed
⅓ cup pine nuts, toasted (page 16)
2 tablespoons minced fresh parsley leaves
2 tablespoons minced fresh basil leaves

1. Scoop out the zucchini flesh, keeping about ¼ inch of flesh and the shells intact. Chop the pulp.

2. Heat 1 tablespoon of the olive oil in a medium-size skillet over medium heat, add the shallots, garlic, and chopped zucchini, and season with salt and pepper to taste. Cover and cook until the vegetables are tender, about 10 minutes. Stir in the tomato, beans, pine nuts, parsley, and basil, season to taste with salt and pepper, and mix well.

3. Fill the zucchini shells with the stuffing mixture and place them in a lightly oiled 5½- to 6-quart oval slow cooker. Drizzle the zucchini with the remaining 1 tablespoon oil. Cover and cook on Low for 3 to 4 hours, until the zucchini is tender.

Chipotle Rice–Stuffed Zucchini

The smoky hot flavor of chipotle chiles enlivens the rice stuffing, which is also delicious stuffed in bell peppers and other vegetables. Chipotle chiles are available dried or canned in a spicy tomato sauce, called adobo. Either can be used in this recipe; if using dried, however, the chiles need to be softened in hot water before puréeing.

Slow Cooker Size:
5½ to 6 quart oval

Cook Time: 3 to 4 hours

Setting: Low

Serves 4

4 small or 2 large zucchini, halved and ends trimmed
2 tablespoons olive oil
1 small yellow onion, minced
1 small carrot, grated
Salt and freshly ground black pepper
1 teaspoon ground cumin
2 cups cooked white or brown rice
1 chipotle chile, puréed

1. Scoop out the zucchini flesh, keeping about ¼ inch of the flesh and the shells intact. Place the zucchini shells, cut side up, in a lightly oiled 5½- to 6-quart oval slow cooker. Chop the pulp.

2. Heat 1 tablespoon of the olive oil in a large skillet over medium heat, add the onion, carrot, and chopped zucchini, and season with salt and pepper to taste. Cover and cook until softened, about 5 minutes. Add the cumin, rice, and chipotle purée, season with salt and pepper to taste, and mix well.

3. Spoon the stuffing mixture evenly into the zucchini. Drizzle with the remaining 1 tablespoon oil. Cover and cook on Low 3 to 4 hours, until the zucchini is tender. Serve hot.

Bulgur and Lentil–Stuffed Eggplant

This recipe requires a 5½- to 6-quart oval slow cooker in order to accommodate the eggplant stuffed with hearty and nutritious bulgur and lentils. Best known for its use in tabbouleh, bulgur is a quick-cooking grain made from wheat kernels that have been steamed, dried, and crushed. Available in natural food stores, well-stocked supermarkets, and specialty grocers, bulgur has a robust flavor and chewy texture.

Slow Cooker Size:
5½ to 6 quart oval

Cook Time: 4 to 5 hours

Setting: Low

Serves 4

1 large eggplant, halved lengthwise
2 tablespoons olive oil
1 small yellow onion, chopped
1 small carrot, grated
2 garlic cloves, minced
1 jalapeño chile (optional), seeded and minced
1 cup cooked lentils, drained
1 cup cooked bulgur
Salt and freshly ground black pepper
One 14.5-ounce can crushed tomatoes
1 tablespoon chili powder
1 teaspoon peeled and grated fresh ginger
½ cup water

1. Scoop out the inside of the eggplant, leaving ¼ to ⅓ inch of the flesh and the shells intact and set aside. Coarsely chop the eggplant flesh.

2. Heat the oil in a large skillet over medium heat. Add the onion, carrot, chopped eggplant, garlic, and jalapeño, if using; cover, and cook until softened, about 5 minutes, then transfer to a large mixing bowl.

3. To the same bowl, add the lentils and bulgur and season with salt and pepper to taste. Mix well, then stuff the mixture evenly into the eggplant shells. Arrange the eggplant halves in a 5½- to 6-quart oval slow cooker.

4. In the same bowl, combine the tomatoes, chili powder, ginger, and water, season with salt and pepper to taste, blend well, then pour the sauce on and around the eggplants. Cover and cook on Low until the eggplant shells are tender but still hold their shape, 4 to 5 hours. Serve hot.

Vidalia Onions with Shiitake-Hoisin Stuffing

The sweetness of the onions is enhanced by the hoisin sauce and complemented by the woodsy flavor of the shiitakes. Be sure the onions fit in your slow cooker if it is smaller than $5\frac{1}{2}$ to 6 quart. (With a smaller cooker, you may need to use fewer onions.)

Slow Cooker Size:
$5\frac{1}{2}$ to 6 quart

Cook Time: 6 hours

Setting: Low

Serves 4

4 large Vidalia or other sweet yellow onions, peeled
1 tablespoon peanut oil
6 ounces fresh shiitake mushrooms, stemmed and caps chopped
1 tablespoon tamari or other soy sauce
$\frac{1}{4}$ cup hoisin sauce
1 tablespoon toasted sesame oil
1 cup dry bread crumbs
1 cup hot water

1. Slice off the tops of the onions and hollow out, leaving about a $\frac{1}{2}$-inch-thick shell. Chop enough of the onion centers to yield $\frac{1}{2}$ cup.

2. Heat the oil in a large skillet over medium heat. Add the chopped onion, cover, and cook until softened, about 5 minutes. Add the mushrooms and cook until softened, about 3 minutes. Add the tamari, 2 tablespoons of the hoisin sauce, and the sesame oil, then stir in the bread crumbs until well combined.

3. Spoon the stuffing into the hollowed-out onion shells and place them in a $5\frac{1}{2}$- to 6-quart slow cooker.

4. Place the remaining 2 tablespoons hoisin sauce in a small bowl. Add the water, stirring to blend, then pour the liquid around the onions. Cover and cook on Low for 6 hours, until the onions are tender.

Rice and Raisin–Stuffed Cabbage Rolls

Plump raisins, apple juice, and a bit of sugar and spice lend a sweetness to these flavorful cabbage bundles made with nutritious and nutty brown rice.

Slow Cooker Size:
5½ to 6 quart

Cook Time: 6 to 8 hours

Setting: Low

Serves 4 to 6

1 large head green cabbage, cored
2 tablespoons olive oil
1 medium-size yellow onion, chopped
½ cup raisins, soaked in warm water 10 minutes and drained
2 tablespoons minced fresh parsley leaves
1 teaspoon sugar or a natural sweetener
¼ teaspoon ground allspice
⅛ teaspoon ground cinnamon
⅛ teaspoon cayenne pepper
Salt and freshly ground black pepper
3 cups cooked brown rice
1 tablespoon fresh lemon juice
¾ cup water
¾ cup apple juice

1. Steam the cabbage in a large pot with a steamer rack until the first few layers of leaves are softened, about 10 minutes. Remove from the pot and allow to cool.

2. Heat 1 tablespoon of the olive oil in a large skillet over medium heat. Add the onion, cover, and cook until softened, about 5 minutes. Add the raisins, parsley, sugar, allspice, and cinnamon, season with cayenne, salt, and black pepper, and mix well. Remove from the heat, stir in the rice and lemon juice, and mix well.

3. Remove as many of the cabbage leaves that are soft and lay them out on flat surface, rib side down. Place about ⅓ cup of the stuffing mixture on each leaf. Roll up each leaf around the stuffing, tucking in the sides as you roll. Repeat the process until the mixture is used up, steaming more cabbage leaves to soften as necessary.

4. Place the filled cabbage rolls in a 5½- to 6-quart slow cooker, seam side down. Drizzle with the remaining 1 tablespoon olive oil, the water, and apple juice. Cover and cook on Low for 6 to 8 hours, until the cabbage is tender. Serve hot.

Tempeh and Barley–Stuffed Cabbage Rolls

Known as *halupki* in Slovak and *galumpki* in Polish, these cabbage rolls are typically stuffed with rice or barley and ground meat. Here I use barley with tempeh, but you could easily substitute a different cooked grain for the barley or use vegetarian burger crumbles instead of the tempeh.

Slow Cooker Size:
5½ to 6 quart

Cook Time: 6 to 8 hours

Setting: Low

Serves 4 to 6

1 large head green cabbage, cored
1 tablespoon olive oil
1 medium-size yellow onion, grated
1 small carrot, grated
12 ounces tempeh, finely chopped
2½ cups cooked barley
½ teaspoon dillweed
Salt and freshly ground black pepper
One 14.5-ounce can crushed tomatoes
⅓ cup sugar or a natural sweetener
¼ cup cider vinegar

1. Steam the cabbage in a large covered pot with a steamer rack until the first few layers of leaves are softened, about 10 minutes. Remove the cabbage from the pot and allow to cool.

2. Heat the olive oil in a large skillet over medium heat. Add the onion and carrot, cover, and cook until softened, about 10 minutes. Stir in the tempeh and cook 5 minutes longer. Remove from the heat, add the barley and dillweed, and season with salt and pepper to taste. Mix well.

3. Remove as many of the cabbage leaves that are soft and lay them out on a flat surface, rib side down. Place about ⅓ cup of the stuffing mixture in the center of each leaf. Roll up the leaf around the stuffing, folding in the sides as you roll. Repeat the process until the stuffing mixture is used up, steaming more cabbage leaves to soften if necessary. Arrange the filled cabbage rolls in a 5½- to 6-quart slow cooker, seam side down.

4. In a medium-size mixing bowl, combine the tomatoes, sugar, and vinegar and season with salt and pepper to taste. Pour over the cabbage rolls. Cover and cook on Low for 6 to 8 hours, until the rolls are tender. Serve hot.

Yuba-Wrapped Vegetarian Haggis

Yuba, or bean curd skin, available in Asian markets where it is sold fresh or frozen in large sheets, is a versatile ingredient often used as a dumpling wrapper. Here it is a crispy outer wrapper for a flavorful vegetarian version of a Scottish classic, traditionally served with mashed potatoes and mashed rutabaga (called "swede" in Scotland) on January 25th—Robert Burns's birthday.

Slow Cooker Size:
4 quart

Cook Time: 4 hours

Setting: Low

Serves 4

2 tablespoons olive oil

1 large yellow onion, chopped

2 large carrots, finely shredded

4 ounces white mushrooms, chopped

1¾ cups vegetable stock (see A Note About Stock, page 32)

¾ cup rolled (old-fashioned) oats

1½ cups slow-cooked (page 95) or one 15.5-ounce can kidney beans, drained and rinsed

⅔ cup chopped pecans or other nuts

2 tablespoons minced fresh parsley leaves

2 tablespoons Scotch whiskey (optional)

1½ tablespoons tamari or other soy sauce

1½ teaspoons dried thyme

⅛ teaspoon ground nutmeg

⅛ teaspoon cayenne pepper

Salt and freshly ground black pepper

1 large sheet fresh or frozen bean curd skin (*yuba*), thawed if necessary

1. Heat the oil in a large saucepan over medium heat. Add the onion and carrots, cover, and cook until softened, about 5 minutes. Add the mushrooms and stock, stir in the oats, reduce heat to low, and simmer, uncovered, for 10 minutes.

2. Mash or coarsely chop the kidney beans and stir into the oat mixture. Add the nuts, parsley, whiskey (if using), tamari, thyme, nutmeg, and cayenne and season with salt and black pepper to taste. Mix well to combine.

3. The bean curd skin should be soft, not brittle. If it is brittle, soak in a shallow bowl of water for a few seconds to soften. Line a lightly oiled 4-quart slow cooker with the *yuba* and spoon the stuffing mixture inside. Fold the *yuba* sheet over onto the mixture to enclose it. Cover and cook on Low for 4 hours.

4. To serve, cut it into quarters using a sharp knife, then spoon portions out using a large spoon. Serve hot.

Note: If you can't find bean curd skin, the recipe can be made without it—just spoon the stuffing mixture directly into the lightly oiled cooker insert and proceed with the recipe. The stuffing is also delicious cooked inside a kabocha or other large winter squash.

Doneness Factors in the Slow Cooker

In addition to cooking on High or Low, the amount of time it will take for food to cook depends on many factors, such as:

- The size of the pieces of vegetables and other ingredients you are using.

- The amount of liquid in the pot. Hint: If you use hot or boiling liquid, it will shorten the cooking time.

- The temperature of the ingredients to start with. If your ingredients are room temperature, they will cook faster than if the ingredients (or the entire ceramic cooking insert) just came out of the refrigerator.

- The type and model of slow cooker. Some slow cookers are calibrated differently from others so that one's Low may be several degrees hotter than another. I have discovered that one of my slow cookers cooks "faster" (or hotter) than the others and so I plan accordingly.

Savory Stuffed Wheat-Meat Roast with Quick Mushroom Gravy

This delicious roast makes enough to serve a crowd and is especially good with gravy and mashed potatoes. Use the recipe for Seitan from Scratch up to the point before poaching it or use Seitan Quick Mix, available through natural food stores, to make a quick batch.

Slow Cooker Size:
6 quart oval

Cook Time: 6 to 8 hours

Setting: Low

Serves 8

One 1-pound piece raw, unpoached seitan (page 129)
½ cup tamari or other soy sauce
2 tablespoons olive oil
1 small yellow onion, minced
½ cup minced celery
1 teaspoon dried thyme
1 teaspoon ground sage
6 cups ½-inch bread cubes
8 ounces cooked soy sausage, crumbled or coarsely chopped
2 tablespoons minced fresh parsley leaves
1 teaspoon salt
¼ teaspoon freshly ground black pepper
About ½ cup water
¾ cup water combined with 1 tablespoon tamari or other soy sauce
Quick Mushroom Gravy (recipe follows)

1. In a zipper-top plastic bag, marinate the raw seitan in the tamari for 30 minutes at room temperature or overnight in the refrigerator.

2. Heat the oil in a large skillet over medium heat. Add the onion and celery, cover, and cook until softened, 5 to 7 minutes. Stir in the thyme and sage and remove from the heat.

3. In a large mixing bowl, combine the cubed bread, sausage, parsley, salt, pepper, and onion mixture and mix well. Taste and the adjust seasonings, adding just enough of the water to moisten. Set aside.

4. Drain and pat dry the seitan, then roll it out with a rolling pin on a work surface to about ¼ inch thick. Spread the surface with the stuffing and roll it up. Tie with kitchen string if necessary.

5. Place the roast, seam side down, in a lightly oiled 6-quart oval slow cooker. Pierce the roast with a fork in several places, then pour the

water-and-tamari mixture over the roast. Cover and cook on Low for 6 to 8 hours.

6. Carefully remove the roast from the slow cooker and let stand for 10 minutes before slicing. Use a serrated knife to cut the roast into ½-inch-thick slices. Serve hot with the gravy.

Quick Mushroom Gravy

Vegetarian browning liquids such as Gravy Master are available in supermarkets and are used to deepen the color of the gravy to a rich brown.

2 cups water
1 cup coarsely chopped white mushrooms
3 tablespoons tamari or other soy sauce
1 teaspoon dried thyme
Salt and freshly ground black pepper
1½ tablespoons cornstarch dissolved in 3 tablespoons water
1 teaspoon Gravy Master or other vegetarian browning liquid

1. In a small saucepan, combine the water, mushrooms, tamari, and thyme, season with salt and pepper to taste, and bring to a boil. Reduce the heat to low and simmer for 3 minutes to soften mushrooms.

2. Transfer the mixture to a blender or food processor and process until smooth. Return the mixture to the saucepan over high heat and bring to a boil. Reduce the heat to low, whisk in the cornstarch mixture, and stir until the sauce thickens, 1 to 2 minutes. Stir in the Gravy Master. Taste to adjust the seasonings. Serve hot.

Makes 2½ cups

Cheesy Garlic-Stuffed Artichokes

Make as many artichokes as will fit comfortably in your slow cooker—I use a 5½-quart cooker to hold four large artichokes.

Slow Cooker Size:
5½ to 6 quart

Cook Time: 4 hours

Setting: Low

Serves 4

2 tablespoons olive oil

3 garlic cloves, minced

12 ounces soy sausage, crumbled

3 cups dry bread crumbs

⅓ cup freshly grated Parmesan cheese or soy Parmesan

3 tablespoons chopped fresh parsley leaves

Cayenne pepper

Salt and freshly ground black pepper

4 large artichokes

Juice of 2 lemons

2 cups water

1. Heat 1 tablespoon of the oil in a large skillet over medium heat. Add the garlic and cook until fragrant, about 30 seconds. Stir in the sausage and cook for 5 minutes, stirring to blend. Remove from the heat, stir in the bread crumbs, cheese, and parsley, and season with cayenne, salt, and black pepper to taste. Mix well and set aside.

2. Slice off the stem end of each artichoke so that they sit upright. Cut about an inch off the top of each artichoke and, with scissors, snip off any sharp tips from the artichoke leaves. In a bowl, combine half of the lemon juice with the water and dip the cut artichokes into the lemon water to prevent browning. Spread the leaves of each artichoke as much as possible and place as much of the stuffing mixture in between the artichoke leaves, pressing it in with your fingers.

3. Stand the stuffed artichokes in a slow cooker large enough to hold them in a single layer. Pour about 1 inch of water into the bottom of the cooker. Drizzle each artichoke with the remaining 1 tablespoon olive oil and remaining lemon juice. Cover and cook on Low for 4 hours, until the leaves pull off easily and are tender. Serve hot or at room temperature.

Vegetables

· · ·

In addition to its talent for cooking soups, stews, and bean dishes, the slow cooker is also well suited to making a variety of vegetables. Hard winter vegetables such as potatoes, carrots, parsnips, beets, and winter squash all benefit from slow cooking, as do many other vegetables, including celery, tomatoes, cabbage, and onions.

This chapter offers a wide variety of slow-simmered vegetable dishes, such as Half-Day Ratatouille (page 171), Balsamic-Braised Root Vegetables (page 182), and Sweet-and-Sour Cipollini Onions with Walnuts and Golden Raisins (page 186).

The slow cooker also can be used to make casseroles, such as Sweet Potato Casserole with Pineapple and Coconut (page 180) or Green Bean and White Bean Casserole (page 185). It can even be enlisted to prepare baked potatoes and corn on the cob on those summer days when you don't want to heat the kitchen. This chapter is loaded with side dishes that will convince you to own two cookers—a larger one for main courses and a smaller one for sides.

Half-Day Ratatouille

Slow cooking brings out the flavors of the vegetables in this mélange inspired by the classic Provençal dish. Enjoy ratatouille as a side dish or serve over rice or pasta for a delicious entrée.

Slow Cooker Size:
3½ to 4 quart

Cook Time: 4 hours

Setting: Low

Serves 4 to 6

2 tablespoons olive oil
1 small eggplant, cut into ½-inch dice
1 small yellow onion, diced
1 small red bell pepper, seeded and cut into ½-inch dice
2 garlic cloves, minced
2 small zucchini, cut into ½-inch-thick rounds
One 28-ounce can diced tomatoes, with their juice
1 teaspoon dried thyme
Salt and freshly ground black pepper
3 tablespoons pesto, homemade (page 51) or store-bought

1. Heat 1 tablespoon of the oil in a large skillet over medium heat. Add the eggplant and cook, stirring, until softened, about 5 minutes. Using a slotted spoon, transfer the eggplant to a 3½- to 4-quart slow cooker.

2. Add the remaining 1 tablespoon oil to the same skillet over medium heat. Add the onion, cover, and cook until softened, about 5 minutes. Add the onion to the slow cooker along with the bell pepper, garlic, zucchini, tomatoes and their juice, and thyme. Season with salt and pepper. Cover and cook on Low for 4 hours, until the vegetables are tender.

3. Just before serving, stir in the pesto.

Vegetable Tian with Herbes de Provence

This country French vegetable casserole is traditionally slow cooked in an earthenware baking dish also called a *tian*, so preparing it in a slow cooker is a natural alternative. *Herbes de Provence* is a mixture of dried herbs available at gourmet markets and specialty food shops. If the herb mixture is unavailable, you can approximate it by using a combination of three parts dried marjoram, thyme, and savory to one part basil, rosemary, tarragon, and fennel seeds.

Slow Cooker Size:
3½ to 4 quart

Cook Time: 6 to 8 hours

Setting: Low

Serves 4 to 6

6 shallots, halved
2 large garlic cloves, minced
1½ cups baby carrots
1 pound small red potatoes, quartered
1 small red bell pepper, seeded and diced
1½ cups cherry tomatoes, halved
¼ cup vegetable stock (see A Note About Stock, page 32) or water
3 tablespoons olive oil
1½ teaspoons dried *herbes de Provence*
Salt and freshly ground black pepper
1 cup fresh bread crumbs

1. Combine all the vegetables in a 3½- to 4-quart slow cooker. Add the vegetable stock and 2 tablespoons of the olive oil. Season with the *herbes de Provence* and salt and pepper. Combine well to coat the vegetables. Cover and cook on Low for 6 to 8 hours.

2. In a small skillet, toast the bread crumbs in the remaining 1 tablespoon olive oil over medium heat until golden brown. Set aside.

3. When the *tian* is done, sprinkle the bread crumb mixture over the top and serve.

"Messa" Collards

Collard greens are popular in the southern states, where they are often cooked for hours on top of the stove. A slow cooker is just the thing to cook a "messa" collards without standing over the pot. Wash the collards well to remove all traces of sand and grit. Liquid Smoke, available in supermarkets, adds a nice depth of flavor to the collards.

Slow Cooker Size:
3½ to 4 quart

Cook Time: 6 hours

Setting: Low

Serves 4

1 tablespoon olive oil

1 small yellow onion, chopped

1 large garlic clove, minced

1 pound fresh collard greens, trimmed of heavy stems, well washed, and coarsely chopped

1 cup vegetable stock (see A Note About Stock, page 32) or water

Salt and freshly ground black pepper

1½ tablespoons cider vinegar or 1 teaspoon Liquid Smoke

1. Pour the oil into a 3½- to 4-quart slow cooker. Set the heat on High, add the onion and garlic, cover, and cook while you prep the remaining ingredients.

2. Once prepped, add the collards and stock to the slow cooker and season with salt and pepper. Change the heat setting to Low, cover, and cook for 6 hours, until the collards are tender.

3. Just before serving, stir in the vinegar or Liquid Smoke.

Slow-Baked Potatoes

Foil-wrapped baking potatoes create their own steam as they cook gently in the slow cooker. The size of the potatoes will determine the length of cooking time needed. When you think the potatoes might be ready, test them with a fork to see if they are tender. If the fork passes through easily, they're done.

Slow Cooker Size:
4 to 6 quart

Cook Time: 6 to 8 hours

Setting: Low

Serves 4

4 russet or other baking potatoes, well scrubbed but not dried

1. Prick the potatoes with a fork and wrap them individually in aluminum foil.

2. Place the foil-wrapped potatoes in a 4- to 6-quart slow cooker, cover, and cook on Low for 6 to 8 hours, until soft.

Two's Company

If you think that having one slow cooker is convenient, then you will find that having two will definitely double your pleasure. As many slow cooker fans have discovered, there is frequently a need for both a smaller and larger cooker—often at the same time. Sometimes you may need a large one for the main dish and the smaller one for a side dish, soup, or dessert. I actually have three—one small round, one large round, and one large oval—and they all get a lot of use, especially when I have one of my marathon cooking days, usually a Sunday, when my husband and I storm the kitchen and chop everything in sight. We end up making meals for several days that week, as well as some we freeze for future use. But even if it's just to take advantage of the various recipes that are best prepared in one size or another, you may want to consider buying a second cooker.

Rustic Mashed Potatoes with Garlic

The slow cooker is an easy and convenient way to make mashed potatoes. Not only can you make and serve them in the same container, but they will keep warm in the cooker while you finish preparing the rest of the meal.

Slow Cooker Size:
3½ to 4 quart

Cook Time: 4 to 5 hours

Setting: Low

Serves 4

1 tablespoon olive oil

3 large garlic cloves, smashed

1½ pounds Yukon Gold or russet potatoes, left unpeeled, well scrubbed, and cut into 2-inch chunks

½ cup vegetable stock (see A Note About Stock, page 32)

¼ cup heated milk or soy milk

Salt and freshly ground black pepper

1. Spread the oil in the bottom of a 3½- to 4-quart slow cooker. Add the garlic and potatoes. Pour the stock over the potatoes, cover, and cook on Low 4 to 5 hours, until tender.

2. When the potatoes are soft, add the milk and season to taste with salt and pepper. Using a potato masher, mash the potatoes and garlic until all the ingredients are incorporated. Some lumps may remain. Serve hot.

Layered Pesto Potatoes with Sun-Dried Tomatoes

Pesto and sun-dried tomatoes join forces with buttery Yukon Gold potatoes for a dish that can be enjoyed as an entrée or a side.

Slow Cooker Size:
3½ to 4 quart

Cook Time: 6 hours

Setting: Low

Serves 4 to 6

3 tablespoons olive oil
1 medium-size yellow onion, minced
2 garlic cloves, minced
⅓ cup oil-packed or reconstituted sun-dried tomatoes, drained and chopped
1½ pounds Yukon Gold or other all-purpose potatoes, peeled and cut into ¼-inch-thick slices
Salt and freshly ground black pepper
½ cup pesto, homemade (page 51) or store-bought
½ cup fresh bread crumbs

1. Heat 2 tablespoons of the oil in a large skillet over medium heat. Add the onion, cover, and cook until softened, about 5 minutes. Stir in the garlic and sun-dried tomatoes and cook 1 minute longer; set aside.

2. Lightly oil a 3½- to 4-quart slow cooker. Arrange one half of the potatoes in the bottom of the insert. Top with half of the onion mixture. Season with salt and pepper and dot with half of the pesto. Top with a layer of the remaining potatoes, the remaining onion mixture, and the remaining pesto and season with salt and pepper. Cover and cook on Low for 6 hours, until the potatoes are tender.

3. In a small skillet, toast the bread crumbs in the remaining 1 tablespoon olive oil over medium heat until golden brown. Set aside.

4. When ready to serve, top evenly with the bread crumbs.

New Potatoes, Fennel, and Radicchio with Kalamata Olives and Basil

Two Mediterranean favorites, fennel and radicchio, combine with potatoes for a simply sublime vegetable mélange that is accented by fragrant basil and the salty flavor of Kalamata olives. If using tiny creamer potatoes, you can leave them whole, but if your potatoes are larger, you will need to halve or quarter them.

Slow Cooker Size:
4 quart

Cook Time: 5 to 6 hours

Setting: Low

Serves 4

1 pound small red or white potatoes, whole, halved, or quartered
1 medium-size fennel bulb, stalks discarded and quartered
1 small head radicchio, quartered
4 garlic cloves, crushed
3 tablespoons olive oil
Salt and freshly ground black pepper
½ cup pitted Kalamata olives, drained
3 tablespoons chopped fresh basil leaves

1. Combine the potatoes, fennel, radicchio, and garlic in a 4-quart slow cooker. Add the olive oil and salt and pepper and stir to combine and coat with the oil. Cover and cook on Low for 5 to 6 hours, until the vegetables are tender.

2. Just before serving, add the olives and basil and toss to combine.

Slow-Baked Sweet Potatoes

The moisture remaining after washing the sweet potatoes adds a bit of steam, which will help cook the potatoes. Cooking time will vary, depending on the size and shape of the potatoes. When you think the potatoes might be ready, test them with a fork to see if they are tender. If the fork passes through easily, they're done.

Slow Cooker Size:
4 to 6 quart

Cook Time: 4 to 6 hours

Setting: Low

Serves 4

4 medium-size sweet potatoes

Wash the sweet potatoes well, drain them, but do not dry them. Place in a 4- to 6-quart slow cooker. Cover and cook on Low for 4 to 6 hours, until soft.

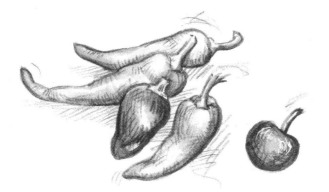

Smashed Sweet Potatoes with Dried Cranberries

The sweet-tart addition of cranberries adds a burst of color and flavor to sweet potatoes, which will make this dish a new family favorite. This slow cooker recipe is especially practical for holiday dinners, when you never seem to have enough burners on the stove or room in the oven.

Slow Cooker Size:
3½ to 4 quart

Cook Time: 6 hours

Setting: Low

Serves 4 to 6

4 large sweet potatoes, peeled and cut into ½-inch-thick slices
½ cup apple juice
¼ cup firmly packed light brown sugar
Salt and freshly ground black pepper
⅓ cup sweetened dried cranberries

1. Place the sweet potatoes slices in a lightly oiled 3½- to 4-quart slow cooker. In a small bowl combine the apple juice and brown sugar and pour over the potatoes. Season with salt and pepper. Cover and cook on Low for 6 hours, until the potatoes are tender.

2. Just before serving, smash the potatoes with a potato masher until smooth, then fold in the cranberries. Serve hot.

Sweet Potato Casserole with Pineapple and Coconut

As the shredded sweet potatoes soften, they blend with the luscious flavors of coconut and pineapple for a slow-cooked casserole with a taste of the tropics.

Slow Cooker Size:
3½ to 4 quart

Cook Time: 6 hours

Setting: Low

Serves 4 to 6

2 pounds sweet potatoes, peeled and shredded
¼ cup firmly packed light brown sugar
¼ cup unsweetened shredded coconut
¼ teaspoon ground cinnamon
½ cup chopped fresh or canned pineapple
¼ teaspoon pure coconut extract
¼ teaspoon pure vanilla extract

1. Lightly oil the insert of a 3½- to 4-quart slow cooker. Add the sweet potatoes, brown sugar, coconut, and cinnamon and stir to combine. Cover and cook on Low for 6 hours.

2. Shortly before serving, stir in the pineapple and extracts.

Maple-Glazed Winter Squash with Garlic and Ginger

I enjoy making this dish for the lovely aroma it shares with the house while it cooks. Butternut squash is used in this recipe because it peels more easily than other winter squashes. However, you can use an unpeeled kabocha or buttercup squash if you prefer—just scrub the outside well.

Slow Cooker Size:
3½ to 4 quart

Cook Time: 6 hours

Setting: Low

Serves 4

2 tablespoons olive oil
1 small yellow onion, thinly sliced
2 large garlic cloves, thinly sliced
One 1-inch piece fresh ginger, peeled and thinly sliced
2 tablespoons water
1 tablespoon tamari or other soy sauce
1 large butternut squash, halved, seeded, and peeled
⅓ cup pure maple syrup
2 tablespoons firmly packed light brown sugar or a natural sweetener
Salt and freshly ground black pepper

1. Spread the oil in the bottom of a 3½- to 4-quart slow cooker. Arrange the onion slices over the oil, followed by the garlic and ginger. Combine the water and tamari and add to the cooker.

2. Cut the squash into 2-inch chunks and place them on top of the vegetables in the cooker. Pour the maple syrup over the squash, sprinkle with the brown sugar, and season with salt and pepper.

3. Cover and cook on Low for 6 hours, until the squash is soft. Serve hot.

Balsamic-Braised Root Vegetables

Slow cooking combined with balsamic vinegar and sugar brings out the natural sweetness of root vegetables.

Slow Cooker Size:
3½ to 4 quart

Cook Time: 8 hours

Setting: Low

Serves 4

3 large carrots, cut into 1-inch chunks
4 shallots, halved
2 small turnips, peeled and cut into 1-inch cubes
1 large parsnip, peeled and cut into 1-inch pieces
2 tablespoons olive oil
2 tablespoons balsamic vinegar
2 tablespoons water
1 tablespoon firmly packed light brown sugar
Salt and freshly ground black pepper

1. Place the carrots, shallots, turnips, and parsnip in a 3½- to 4-quart slow cooker.

2. In a small bowl, combine the oil, vinegar, water, and sugar. Pour over the vegetables and season with salt and pepper. Stir to combine.

3. Cover and cook on Low for 8 hours, until the vegetables are soft. Stir once about halfway through, if possible.

Three Orange–Flavored Beets

Orange marmalade, orange juice concentrate, and fresh orange juice team up to infuse the beets with citrus sweetness. Use the smallest beets you can find for the best flavor.

Slow Cooker Size:
3½ to 4 quart

Cook Time: 6 to 8 hours

Setting: Low

Serves 4

2 tablespoons orange marmalade
2 tablespoons frozen orange juice concentrate, thawed
Juice of 1 orange
2 tablespoons extra virgin olive oil
8 to 10 small fresh beets, trimmed, well scrubbed, and halved, or
    4 large beets, quartered
Salt and freshly ground black pepper

1. In a small bowl, combine the marmalade, orange juice concentrate, and orange juice. Add the oil, stirring to blend.

2. Place the beets in a 3½- to 4-quart slow cooker and add the orange mixture, stirring to coat. Season with salt and pepper. Cover and cook on Low for 6 to 8 hours, stirring once halfway through if possible, until the beets are soft.

3. Before serving, remove the beet peels (they should come off easily) and place the beets in a serving bowl. Pour the orange mixture over the beets before serving.

Provençal Green Beans

These green beans, simmered in a fragrant mixture of tomatoes, onions, and garlic, are delicious as a side dish or as a topping for pasta, rice, or baked potatoes.

Slow Cooker Size:
3½ to 4 quart

Cook Time: 5 to 6 hours

Setting: Low

Serves 4

2 tablespoons olive oil
1 small yellow onion, minced
2 garlic cloves, minced
1 pound green beans, ends trimmed and cut into 1-inch pieces
One 14.5-ounce can diced tomatoes, drained
Salt and freshly ground black pepper

1. Pour the oil into a 3½- to 4-quart slow cooker set on High. Add the onion and garlic, cover, and cook to soften slightly while you assemble and prep the remaining ingredients.

2. Once prepped, add the green beans and tomatoes, season with salt and pepper, and stir to combine. Cover, change the heat setting to Low, and cook for 5 to 6 hours, until the beans are tender.

Green Bean and White Bean Casserole

The white beans are puréed to make a creamy and flavorful sauce for the green beans. Instead of the toasted almond topping, you could go retro and top the beans with a can of French's Fried Onion Rings. Another alternate topping idea is toasted bread crumbs and shredded regular or soy mozzarella.

Slow Cooker Size:
3½ to 4 quart

Cook Time: 4 to 6 hours

Setting: Low

Serves 4

1 tablespoon olive oil
1 small yellow onion, chopped
1 cup chopped white mushrooms
2 garlic cloves, minced
1½ cups slow-cooked (page 95) or one 15.5-ounce can white beans, drained and rinsed
1 cup water
Salt and freshly ground black pepper to taste
1½ pounds green beans, ends trimmed and cut into 1-inch pieces
½ cup sliced almonds, toasted (see below)

1. Heat the oil in a large skillet over medium-high heat, add the onion, cover, and cook until softened, about 5 minutes. Place the onion mixture in a blender. To the same skillet, add the mushrooms and garlic, and stir until softened over medium-high heat, about 3 minutes. Set aside.

2. Add the white beans and water to the blender with the onion mixture, season with salt and pepper, and process until smooth.

3. Place the green beans and sautéed mushrooms in a 3½- to 4-quart slow cooker and pour the white bean sauce over them. Cover and cook on Low for 4 to 6 hours, until the green beans are tender.

4. When you're ready to serve, sprinkle the beans with the almonds.

Toasting Almonds

Place the almonds in a dry skillet over medium heat and shake or stir constantly until toasted to a light golden brown. Remove from the hot pan immediately or they will continue to darken.

Sweet and Sour Cipollini Onions with Walnuts and Golden Raisins

Small Italian cipollini onions are preferable in this recipe. If unavailable, other small onions or pearl onions may be substituted. If larger than bite-size, halve them lengthwise. If using pearl onions, first plunge them in a pot of boiling water for about 15 seconds, then drain, remove the skin, and trim the root end.

Slow Cooker Size:
3½ to 4 quart

Cook Time: 4 to 5 hours

Setting: Low

Serves 4

2 tablespoons olive oil

1½ pounds cipollini or other small onions, peeled, trimmed, and halved if necessary

3 tablespoons sugar or a natural sweetener

¼ cup balsamic vinegar

½ cup water

⅓ cup golden raisins

1 teaspoon chopped fresh rosemary leaves (optional)

Salt and freshly ground black pepper

⅓ cup chopped walnuts

1. Heat the oil in a large skillet over medium-high heat. Add the onions and cook until golden brown all over, about 8 minutes.

2. Transfer to a 3½- to 4-quart slow cooker and add the sugar, vinegar, water, raisins, and rosemary, if using. Season with salt and pepper. Cover and cook on Low for 4 to 5 hours, until the onions are tender.

3. Just before serving, toss the onions to coat with the sauce and sprinkle with the walnuts. Serve warm or at room temperature.

Slow-Simmered Bok Choy

Simmering the bok choy slowly in a delicious sauce makes it tender and flavorful. Baby bok choy, available in Asian markets and larger supermarkets, has dramatic plate-appeal when halved lengthwise and served intact, though it is quite a bit more expensive. If the larger bok choy is all that is available, substitute one large head and cut it into small pieces—it will still taste fine. Mirin, also known as rice wine, is a sweet Japanese cooking wine available in Asian markets and well-stocked super-markets.

Slow Cooker Size:
5½ to 6 quart

Cook Time: 4 hours

Setting: Low

Serves 4 to 6

2 tablespoons tamari or other soy sauce
1 tablespoon hoisin sauce
1 tablespoon mirin
1 tablespoon water
1 tablespoon peanut oil
1 large garlic clove, minced
1 teaspoon peeled and minced fresh ginger
2 to 3 heads baby bok choy, trimmed and halved lengthwise
3 scallions, thinly sliced

1. In a small bowl, combine the tamari, hoisin, mirin, and water. Set aside.

2. Spread the oil in the bottom of a 5½- to 6-quart slow cooker and turn the heat setting to High. Add the garlic and ginger and arrange the bok choy on top. Sprinkle with the scallions and pour the tamari mixture over all. Change the heat setting to Low, cover, and cook for 4 hours, until the bok choy is tender. Serve hot.

Sweet and Sour Cabbage

The slow-cooked flavor of this cabbage makes it an ideal side dish for a cold weather supper. Turn it into an entrée by browning vegetarian sausage links in a skillet and adding it to the cabbage when ready to serve.

Slow Cooker Size:
3½ to 4 quart

Cook Time: 5 to 6 hours

Setting: Low

Serves 6 to 8

1 tablespoon olive oil

1 small yellow onion, minced

2 tablespoons unbleached all-purpose flour

¼ cup water

¾ cup cider vinegar

½ cup firmly packed light brown sugar or a natural sweetener

1 medium-size head red cabbage, cored and shredded

1 medium-size cooking apple, like Granny Smith or Rome Beauty, peeled, cored, and chopped

Salt and freshly ground black pepper

1. Heat the oil in a small skillet over medium heat. Add the onion, cover, and cook until softened, about 5 minutes. Add the flour and cook, stirring, for 1 minute. Add the water, stirring until smooth.

2. Transfer the onion mixture to a 3½- to 4-quart slow cooker and stir in the vinegar and brown sugar. Add the cabbage and apple, season with salt and pepper, and stir to combine. Cover and cook on Low for 5 to 6 hours, until the cabbage is tender. Taste to adjust the seasonings and serve hot.

Vermouth-Braised Celery

This simple vegetable is simply elegant when slow-braised in vermouth and vegetable stock. Garnish with minced roasted red peppers for a striking color contrast or with toasted slivered almonds for a textural one.

Slow Cooker Size:
4 quart

Cook Time: 3 hours

Setting: Low

Serves 4

1 pound celery hearts
2 tablespoons olive oil
¾ cup vegetable stock (see A Note About Stock, page 32)
¼ cup dry vermouth
Salt and freshly ground black pepper

1. Trim the ends and remove the strings from each stalk of celery.

2. Heat the oil in a large skillet over medium-high heat. Add the celery and cook, turning once, until golden brown, about 5 minutes.

3. Transfer the celery to a 4-quart slow cooker. Add the stock and vermouth and season with salt and pepper. Cover and cook on Low for 3 hours, until the celery is tender but not falling apart. Serve hot.

Stewed Tomatoes

If you have a bumper crop of fresh ripe tomatoes, this is a great way to use some of them. If you use plum tomatoes, you will have less watery results (since they are smaller, use 10 to 12). Otherwise, once the tomatoes are tender, you can remove the lid and cook, uncovered, to reduce the liquid. Serve as a side dish or spoon over pasta or rice. You can also portion and freeze the tomatoes for use in soups or stews. When freezing, be sure to leave about one inch of headroom to allow for expansion. Properly stored in a tightly sealed container, the tomatoes will keep well in the freezer for several months.

Slow Cooker Size:
3½ to 4 quart

Cook Time: 5 to 6 hours

Setting: Low

Serves 6

6 to 8 large ripe tomatoes, cored
1 tablespoon olive oil
1 medium-size yellow onion, chopped
½ cup chopped celery
½ small green bell pepper (optional), seeded and chopped
2 teaspoons sugar, or to taste
1 bay leaf
¾ teaspoon salt, or to taste
⅛ teaspoon freshly ground black pepper

1. Plunge the tomatoes in a pot of boiling water for 15 to 20 seconds, then into ice water to cool quickly. Peel the tomatoes, then cut them into quarters and seed. Transfer to a 3½- to 4-quart slow cooker.

2. Heat the oil in a large skillet over medium heat, add the onion, celery, and bell pepper, if using. Cover, and cook until softened, about 5 minutes. Transfer to the slow cooker. Add the sugar, bay leaf, salt, and pepper and stir to combine. Cover and cook on Low for 5 to 6 hours. Remove the bay leaf before eating.

Slow-Cooked Artichokes

Four small to medium-size artichokes (or six baby artichokes) will fit in a 4-quart slow cooker. For larger artichokes (or more of them), you will need to use a larger cooker.

Slow Cooker Size:
4 quart

Cook Time: 6 to 8 hours

Setting: Low

Serves 4

4 medium-size fresh artichokes
Juice of 1 lemon
3 cups boiling water

1. Cut off about 1 inch from the top of the artichokes. Slice off the stem end and trim the pointy tips from the leaves with a pair of scissors. Place the artichokes upright in a 4-quart slow cooker.

2. Drizzle the lemon juice over the artichokes, then add the water to the cooker. Cover and cook on Low for 6 to 8 hours, until the artichokes are tender. Serve hot or at room temperature.

Slow-Cooking Tips

- If there's too much liquid at the end of cooking time, remove the lid and turn the heat to High to evaporate some of it. Conversely, if there's not enough liquid, add a little more.

- Don't use frozen ingredients in slow cooker recipes. Thaw all frozen items first or the cooking time will be way off.

- Hard vegetables, such as onions and carrots, added raw to soups and braised dishes will soften just fine because of the amount of liquid they are cooking in. However, if these same vegetables are added raw to a stew-type dish, they will remain hard long after the rest of the ingredients are cooked because there is not as much liquid for them to cook in. When using hard vegetables in a stew dish, sauté them first to soften them.

Herb-Infused Corn on the Cob

Because corn on the cob is usually in season in the heat of summer, slow cooking can come in handy when you don't want to heat up the kitchen to cook your corn. Leaving the green husks on and inserting fresh herbs inside allows the flavor of the herbs to steep while the corn gently cooks. This is a great way to use a variety of fresh herbs from the garden. If you don't have fresh herbs, the corn may be cooked without them.

Slow Cooker Size:
5½ to 6 quart

Cook Time: 2 to 4 hours

Setting: Low

Serves 4

8 ears corn
8 to 16 long sprigs thyme, rosemary, basil, or other fresh herbs
½ cup hot water

1. Pull back the green husks from the corn, leaving them attached to the cob. Remove the silk from the corn and rinse the ears under cold running water. Trim the ends of the corn if necessary to fit inside the cooker. Place a stem or two of fresh herbs on the corn and bring the husk back up around the ear to close the herbs inside with the corn.

2. Place the corn upright in a 5½- to 6-quart slow cooker if it is a tall round cooker. If using a shallow oval cooker, lay the corn on its side. Add the hot water, cover, and cook on Low for 2 to 4 hours, until the corn is tender. Serve hot.

Note: The ends of the corn may need to be trimmed in order to fit inside your slow cooker.

Condiments

. . .

Anyone who has ever made a chutney, fruit butter, or similar condiment on top of the stove knows the high risk factor of a scorched pot and the consequential need for stirring and careful monitoring. When you use a slow cooker to make your conserves, vegetable relishes, and applesauce, those problems disappear. Just assemble your ingredients in the cooker, turn it on, and walk away. Hours later you will be richly rewarded with the incomparable fragrance (and taste) of your gently simmered wares.

This chapter contains a selection of flavorful condiments ranging from zesty Green Tomato Chutney (page 197) and Cranberry Cabernet Conserve (page 200) to comforting Homestyle Applesauce (page 201) and Ginger-Pear Butter (page 205).

Slow-Cooked Fresh Pear and Dried Fruit Chutney

The pears should be just ripe, not overripe, and can be any variety you prefer, from Anjou to Bartlett.

Slow Cooker Size:
3½ quart

Cook Time: 3 to 4 hours

Setting: Low

Makes about 4 cups

3 ripe pears, peeled, cored, and cut into chunks
2 cups mixed dried fruit, chopped
½ cup golden raisins
2 scallions, minced
¼ cup sugar or a natural sweetener
2 tablespoons white wine vinegar
2 tablespoons fresh lemon juice
1 teaspoon grated lemon zest
1 teaspoon chopped crystallized ginger
¼ teaspoon red pepper flakes (optional)

1. Place all the ingredients in a 3½-quart slow cooker, stirring to combine. Cover and cook on Low for 3 to 4 hours.

2. Remove the lid and let cool completely before storing in the refrigerator in glass jars or other tightly covered containers, where it will keep for several weeks.

Peach-Date Chutney

Fresh peaches are complemented by the sweet dates and pungent ginger for a chutney that is bursting with flavor. Serve this as an accompaniment with seitan or tempeh recipes or with roasted vegetables.

Slow Cooker Size:
3½ quart

Cook Time: 2 to 3 hours

Setting: Low

Makes about 3½ cups

5 large ripe peaches, peeled, pitted and chopped
½ cup chopped pitted dates
2 tablespoons minced onion
½ cup firmly packed light brown sugar or a natural sweetener
¼ cup cider vinegar
1 tablespoon fresh lemon juice
1 teaspoon peeled and grated fresh ginger
½ teaspoon salt
¼ teaspoon red pepper flakes (optional)

1. Place all the ingredients in a 3½-quart slow cooker. Cover and cook on Low for 2 to 3 hours.

2. Remove the lid and let cool completely before storing in the refrigerator in tightly covered containers, where it will keep for 2 to 3 weeks.

Note: Peel peaches the same way you do tomatoes: plunge them into boiling water for about 15 seconds and then into ice water—the skins will remove easily.

Mango-Apple Chutney with Lime

The distinctive, delicious flavors of mango, apple, and lime combine for a zesty chutney that can be enjoyed with a variety of foods, from Indian to Thai. It can also be used to jazz up simple meals such as veggie burgers or rice and beans.

Slow Cooker Size:
3½ quart

Cook Time: 4 hours

Setting: Low

**Makes about
3½ cups**

2 large ripe mangoes, peeled, flesh cut from the seed, and chopped
1 large cooking apple, such as Granny Smith or Rome Beauty, peeled, cored, and chopped
2 large shallots, minced
Juice and grated zest of 2 limes
¾ cup firmly packed light brown sugar or a natural sweetener
½ cup white wine vinegar
1 cinnamon stick

1. Place all the ingredients in a 3½-quart slow cooker. Cover and cook on Low for 4 hours.

2. Remove the lid and let cool completely. Remove the cinnamon stick and store the chutney in the refrigerator in tightly covered containers, where it will keep for several weeks.

Cranberry Cabernet Conserve

A splash of Cabernet wine contributes a deep flavor note to this rich conserve, while the pectin in the apple adds firmness to the texture. Properly stored, the conserve will keep for up to two weeks in the refrigerator.

Slow Cooker Size:
3½ to 4 quart

Cook Time: 4 hours

Setting: Low

Makes about 4 cups

Two 12-ounce bags fresh cranberries, rinsed and picked over for stems
1 large cooking apple, such as Granny Smith or Rome Beauty, cored, left
 unpeeled, and chopped
1½ cups firmly packed light brown sugar or a natural sweetener,
 or more to taste (see Note)
Juice of 1 lemon
1 teaspoon ground cinnamon
½ teaspoon ground allspice
½ cup water
¼ cup Cabernet or other dry red wine

1. Combine all the ingredients in a 3½- to 4-quart slow cooker, stirring to mix. Cover and cook on Low for 4 hours.

2. Remove the lid and let the conserve cool completely. Transfer to glass jars with tight-fitting lids and store in the refrigerator.

Note: The amount of sugar called for in this recipe produces moderately sweet results. Like the bears in the Goldilocks fairy tale, one taster deemed it too sweet, another thought it too tart, and the rest of us thought it was "just right." When you stir this about halfway through, give it a taste, then add a little more sugar at that time, if desired.

Homestyle Applesauce

I like to make this almost as much for the fragrance it gives off while it cooks as for its delicious end results. I prefer a less sweet applesauce and use only $^1/_4$ cup sugar. If you like it sweeter, add more sugar.

Slow Cooker Size:
4 quart

Cook Time: 5 to 6 hours

Setting: Low

Makes about 4 cups

3 pounds large cooking apples, such as Granny Smith or Rome Beauty, peeled, cored, and diced

$^1/_4$ cup sugar or a natural sweetener, or more to taste

$^1/_2$ cup apple juice or water

1 tablespoon fresh lemon juice

1 teaspoon ground cinnamon

$^1/_2$ teaspoon ground allspice

1. Combine all the ingredients in a 4-quart slow cooker. Cover and cook on Low for 5 to 6 hours, until the apples are very soft.

2. Remove the lid and allow to cool completely. Serve at room temperature or transfer to glass jars or other tightly covered containers and refrigerate until ready to use. Properly stored, it will keep for up to 2 weeks.

All-Day Apple Butter

The necessarily long, slow-cooking process of apple butter makes it an ideal candidate for the slow cooker. The apples are left unpeeled to allow the pectin contained in the skin to help thicken the apple butter.

Slow Cooker Size:
4 quart

Cook Time: 10 hours

Setting: 8 hours on Low; 2 hours on High

Makes about 4 cups

3 pounds cooking apples, such as Granny Smith, Rome Beauty, or Gala, cored, left unpeeled, and cut into eighths

¾ cup firmly packed light brown sugar

¾ cup apple juice

Juice of 1 lemon

1 tablespoon ground cinnamon

1 teaspoon ground allspice

½ teaspoon ground nutmeg

¼ teaspoon ground ginger

¼ teaspoon ground cloves

1. Combine the apples, brown sugar, apple juice, and lemon juice in a 4-quart slow cooker. Cover and cook on Low for 8 hours, until the apples are very soft.

2. Remove the lid, turn the heat setting to High, and stir in the spices. Continue to cook, uncovered, for 2 hours, stirring once about halfway through, if possible, until the mixture thickens.

3. Press the apples through a metal strainer into a large mixing bowl to remove the peels, or process the apples through a food mill.

4. After cooling to room temperature, the apple butter may be stored, tightly covered, in the refrigerator in clean jars, where it will keep for several weeks.

Peach Butter

For those fortunate enough to have an abundance of ripe peaches, here's a way to keep a little taste of summer throughout the fall.

Slow Cooker Size:
4 quart

Cook Time: 4 to 6 hours

Setting: Low

Makes about 4 cups

4 pounds ripe peaches, peeled (see Note on page 198), pitted, and diced

1 cup water

⅓ cup firmly packed light brown sugar or a natural sweetener, or more to taste

1 teaspoon fresh lemon juice

½ teaspoon ground ginger

¼ teaspoon ground cloves or allspice

1. Place the peaches and water in a blender or food processor and process until smooth. Transfer to a 4-quart slow cooker and stir in the brown sugar. Cover and cook on Low for 4 to 6 hours.

2. Remove the lid, stir in the lemon juice, ginger, and cloves, and allow to cool, uncovered. Taste to adjust the flavorings. Once cool, the peach butter may be stored in the refrigerator in containers with tight-fitting lids, where it will keep for several weeks.

Pumpkin Butter

This yummy spread is great to have on hand throughout the fall and winter season. Its sweet–savory flavor is delicious with toast and bagels, as well as on tea breads. Be sure to use a small, sweet, pie pumpkin, and not the large, flavorless, jack-o'-lantern variety. A large orange-fleshed winter squash such as buttercup or kabocha may be used instead of a pumpkin. This butter benefits from a good stirring about halfway through the cooking process.

Slow Cooker Size:
3½ to 4 quart

Cook Time: 8 hours

Setting: Low

**Makes about
3 to 4 cups**

1 pie pumpkin, peeled, seeded, and diced
1 small yellow onion, chopped
2 cups apple juice
1 cup firmly packed light brown sugar or a natural sweetener
1 tablespoon ground cinnamon
1 teaspoon ground nutmeg
1 teaspoon ground allspice
1 teaspoon salt

1. In a 3½- to 4-quart slow cooker, combine the pumpkin, onion, apple juice, and brown sugar. Cover and cook on Low for 8 hours, until the pumpkin is very soft.

2. Stir in the spices and salt and mix well. Press the pumpkin mixture through a metal strainer or food mill to achieve a smooth consistency (you could also purée it in a food processor, if you prefer). Let cool to room temperature and store in the refrigerator in tightly covered containers, where it will keep for several weeks.

Ginger-Pear Butter

The flavors of pear and ginger are a match made in heaven, as this simply heavenly fruit butter will attest. It's an interesting change from apple butter—use it as a spread for toast and bagels or even as a topping for pound cake or ice cream. I prefer Anjou or Bartlett pears for this recipe.

Slow Cooker Size:
4 quart

Cook Time: 9 to 10 hours

Setting: 8 hours on Low; 1 to 2 hours on High

Makes about 6 cups

3 pounds ripe pears, peeled, cored, and chopped
¾ cup firmly packed light brown sugar
¾ cup water
1 tablespoon fresh lemon juice
Pinch of salt
1 teaspoon peeled and minced fresh ginger, or to taste
½ teaspoon ground ginger

1. Combine the pears, brown sugar, water, lemon juice, and salt in a 4-quart slow cooker. Cover and cook on Low for 8 hours.

2. Remove the lid and stir in the fresh and ground ginger. Change the heat setting to High and cook, uncovered, to thicken and blend flavors, 1 to 2 hours, stirring occasionally.

3. Let cool completely, then transfer to glass jars or other containers with tight-fitting lids and store in the refrigerator, where it will keep for several weeks.

Desserts from the Slow Cooker

. . .

"Steamed puddings or baked apples, maybe—but cheesecake?" That's the kind of reaction I get when I tell people that I use a slow cooker to make desserts such as cakes, cobblers, and even cheesecakes—all without the hassle of a watched pot or oven.

Making desserts in a slow cooker is almost magical, as the steamy heat of the cooker gently transforms ingredients into tasty "baked" treats. Unlike the dry heat of conventional cooking, the slow cooker produces moist cakes, puddings, and other desserts without the worry of scorching or burning. In addition, I especially enjoy using it to make desserts during the heat of summer, when fresh fruit is at its peak but I don't want to use the oven.

Some desserts, such as the puddings and cobblers, are made right in the cooker insert. Others, such as cakes and cheesecakes, are cooked in baking pans

that are set inside the cooker. Before making a dessert that requires a baking pan to set into your cooker, be sure to find one that fits. I'm partial to using my seven-inch springform pan, which fits inside both my round and oval 6-quart cookers, but there are small cake pans, glass or ceramic baking dishes, and aluminum pans that will work, too. (Some people even use coffee cans.) In addition, there are baking pans available that are especially made to fit inside slow cookers. You will notice that many of the recipes call for a rack or trivet to suspend the cake pan above a small amount of water in the bottom of the cooker. For this purpose, you may use virtually any heatproof object, such as a small bowl, a trivet, a cooling rack, or even a special rack designed to fit inside your slow cooker that may be available from the manufacturer.

Apple-Pecan Spice Cake

This dense, moist cake is especially good served warm to experience the full flavor of the spices. A 6-quart slow cooker is needed for this recipe so that a small baking pan can fit inside. In this and other desserts calling for egg replacement mixture, I recommend Ener-G Egg Replacer, available at natural food stores.

Slow Cooker Size:
6 quart

Cook Time:
3½ to 4 hours

Setting: High

Serves 8

2 cups boiling water
1¾ cups unbleached all-purpose flour
2 teaspoons baking powder
½ teaspoon salt
¼ teaspoon baking soda
⅔ cup firmly packed light brown sugar or a natural sweetener
1 teaspoon ground cinnamon
½ teaspoon ground allspice
¼ teaspoon ground nutmeg
3 medium-size cooking apples, such as Granny Smith or Rome Beauty, peeled, cored, and finely shredded
1 tablespoon fresh lemon juice
1 teaspoon vanilla extract
1 large egg or egg replacement mixture for 1 egg
2 tablespoons corn oil or other mild-tasting oil
½ cup coarsely chopped pecans

1. Place a rack or trivet in a 6-quart slow cooker. Add the boiling water, cover, and turn the heat setting to High. Lightly oil a baking pan that will fit in the cooker and set aside.

2. In a large mixing bowl, sift together the flour, baking powder, salt, and baking soda. Add the brown sugar and spices and stir to combine.

3. In another large mixing bowl, combine the apples and lemon juice, stirring to coat. Stir in the vanilla, egg or egg replacement mixture, and oil. Add the dry mixture to the wet mixture about one-third at a time, mixing well as you go. Fold in the pecans.

4. Transfer the batter to the prepared pan and cover tightly with aluminum foil, making several holes in the foil for steam to escape. Place on the rack, cover, and cook on High for 3½ to 4 hours, until a tester inserted in the center comes out clean.

5. Remove the foil and let cool for 15 minutes before serving.

Spiced Banana Tea Cake with Dried Cherries

This fragrant tea cake is bejeweled with dried cherries, which can be found in well-stocked supermarkets. If unavailable, substitute dried cranberries or golden raisins—or add chopped nuts if you prefer.

Slow Cooker Size:
6 quart

Cook Time:
3½ to 4 hours

Setting: High

Serves 8

2 cups boiling water
1¾ cups unbleached all-purpose flour
2 teaspoons baking powder
¾ teaspoon ground cinnamon
¼ teaspoon ground allspice
⅛ teaspoon ground ginger
⅛ teaspoon ground nutmeg
½ teaspoon salt
⅔ cup sugar or a natural sweetener
3 large ripe bananas, mashed
1 large egg or egg replacement mixture for 1 egg
2 tablespoons corn oil or other mild-tasting oil
1 teaspoon vanilla extract
½ cup chopped dried cherries

1. Place a rack or trivet in a 6-quart slow cooker. Add the boiling water, cover, and turn the heat setting to High. Lightly oil a baking pan that will fit in the cooker and set aside.

2. In a medium-size mixing bowl, sift together the flour, baking powder, spices, and salt. Add the sugar and stir to combine.

3. In a large mixing bowl, combine the bananas, egg or egg replacement, oil, and vanilla. Add the dry mixture to the wet mixture about one-third at a time, mixing well as you go. Fold in the cherries.

4. Transfer the batter to the prepared pan and cover with aluminum foil, making several holes in the foil for steam to escape. Place on the rack, cover, and cook on High for 3½ to 4 hours, until a tester inserted in the center comes out clean.

5. Take the cake out of the cooker, remove the aluminum foil, and let cool for 15 minutes before serving.

Chocolate–Peanut Butter Dream Cake

If you're a fan of those decadent chocolate candies filled with peanut butter, then this cake is your dream come true. Dense chocolate on the inside, it is surrounded by a creamy peanut butter icing. Best of all, since it's made in a slow cooker, there's no worry about burning the cake in the oven, and the gentle cooking ensures a moist cake.

Slow Cooker Size:
6 quart

Cook Time:
3 to 3½ hours

Setting: High

Serves 8

2 cups boiling water

Cake

1½ cups unbleached all-purpose flour
¼ cup unsweetened cocoa powder
2 teaspoons baking powder
¼ teaspoon salt
¼ cup nonhydrogenated margarine, softened
1 cup granulated sugar or a natural sweetener
4 ounces semisweet chocolate, melted
2 large eggs or egg replacement mixture for 2 eggs
1 cup milk or soy milk
1 teaspoon vanilla extract

Icing

2 cups confectioners' sugar
⅔ cup creamy peanut butter (don't use natural)
⅓ cup silken tofu, drained
2 tablespoons softened nonhydrogenated margarine
1 teaspoon vanilla extract

Optional Garnish

1 cup Easy Chocolate Curls (see right)

1. Place a rack or trivet in a 6-quart slow cooker. Add the boiling water, cover, and turn the heat setting to High. Lightly oil a baking pan that will fit in the cooker and set aside.

2. To make the cake, combine the flour, cocoa, baking powder, and salt in a medium-size mixing bowl.

3. In a large mixing bowl with an electric mixer on high speed, cream together the margarine and granulated sugar until blended. Beat in the melted chocolate, eggs or egg replacement mixture, milk, and vanilla until blended. Add the flour mixture and incorporate on low speed until evenly mixed.

4. Transfer the batter to the prepared pan and cover with aluminum foil, making several holes in the foil for steam to escape. Place on the rack, cover, and cook on High for 3 to $3\frac{1}{2}$ hours, until a tester inserted in the center comes out clean.

5. Remove the cake from the slow cooker, remove the foil, and let cool for 15 to 20 minutes, then invert it onto a plate to remove from the pan and cool completely. (If using a springform pan, simply run a knife around the edge of the cake and remove the sides of the pan.)

6. To make the icing, combine the ingredients in a food processor or blender and process until smooth and creamy. Refrigerate at least 1 hour before using to firm up, then ice the cake. Sprinkle the top of the cake with chocolate curls, if using.

Easy Chocolate Curls

The simplest way to make chocolate curls is to warm a piece of chocolate (at least one 1-ounce square) in your hands for a few minutes to soften. Using a vegetable peeler on a flat side of the chocolate, slowly drag it across to make curls. For smaller curls, drag the peeler across the thinner sides of the chocolate. Refrigerate the curls until ready to use so they can firm up.

Chocolate-Coconut Cake

Here's another version of chocolate cake—this time accented with coconut. I use a seven-inch springform pan for this cake (as well as the other cakes in this chapter) and it works great.

Slow Cooker Size:
6 quart

Cook Time:
3 to 3½ hours

Setting: High

Serves 8

2 cups boiling water

Cake

¼ cup nonhydrogenated margarine, softened

1 cup sugar or a natural sweetener

2 large eggs or egg replacement mixture for 2 eggs

1 cup unsweetened coconut milk

1 teaspoon vanilla extract

4 ounces unsweetened chocolate, melted

1½ cups unbleached all-purpose flour

¼ cup unsweetened cocoa powder

2 teaspoons baking powder

¼ teaspoon salt

Icing

½ cup raw unsalted cashews

⅓ cup unsweetened coconut milk

6 ounces silken tofu, drained

¼ cup pure maple syrup

1 teaspoon vanilla extract

1 cup unsweetened shredded coconut

Optional Garnish

1 cup unsweetened shredded coconut, toasted (see right)

1. Place a rack or trivet in a 6-quart slow cooker. Add the boiling water, cover, and turn the heat setting to High. Lightly oil a baking pan that will fit in the cooker and set aside.

2. To make the cake, beat the margarine and sugar together until blended in a large mixing bowl with an electric mixer. Beat in the eggs or egg replacement, coconut milk, vanilla, and melted chocolate until blended.

3. In a medium-size mixing bowl, combine the flour, cocoa, baking powder, and salt. Add to the wet mixture, blending well with an electric mixer on low speed until evenly mixed.

4. Transfer the batter to the prepared pan and cover with aluminum foil, making several holes in the foil for steam to escape. Place the pan on the rack, cover, and cook on High for 3 to $3\frac{1}{2}$ hours, until a tester inserted in the center of the cake comes out clean.

5. Remove the cake from the slow cooker to cool for 15 minutes, then invert onto a plate to remove from the pan and cool completely. (If using a springform pan, simply run a knife around the edge of the cake and remove the sides of the pan.)

6. To make the icing, grind the cashews to a powder in a blender or food processor. Add the coconut milk and blend until smooth. Add the tofu, maple syrup, and vanilla and blend until smooth and creamy. Transfer to a bowl and fold in the coconut. Refrigerate the icing for at least 1 hour before using to firm up.

7. Spread the icing on the cake and sprinkle the top of the cake with the toasted coconut, if using.

How to Toast Coconut

Preheat the oven to 350°F. Spread the shredded coconut on a cookie sheet or shallow baking pan and put in the oven until lightly toasted to a golden brown, stirring occasionally for even browning, about 10 minutes. Let cool to room temperature before using.

Tiramisu-Inspired Tofu Cheesecake

Mascarpone cheese is traditional in tiramisu, but I use tofu and tofu cream cheese to transform the classic dessert into an amazing cholesterol-free cheesecake with bold flavors reminiscent of the classic "pick me up" dessert.

Slow Cooker Size:
6 quart

Cook Time:
2½ to 3 hours

Setting: High

Serves 8

Boiling water as needed

Crust

1½ cups crushed vanilla wafers
¼ cup nonhydrogenated margarine, melted

Cake

8 ounces tofu cream cheese
8 ounces silken tofu, drained
½ cup granulated sugar
1½ tablespoons cornstarch
2 tablespoons strong brewed coffee
2 teaspoons brandy extract
Pinch of salt

Garnish and Sauce

Easy Chocolate Curls (page 213)
½ cup confectioners' sugar
2 tablespoons unsweetened cocoa powder
½ cup strong brewed coffee or espresso, cooled to room temperature
¼ cup brandy

1. Place a rack or trivet in a 6-quart slow cooker. Add the boiling water, cover, and turn the heat setting to High. Lightly oil a springform pan that will fit in the cooker and set aside.

2. To make the crust, combine the crumbs and margarine in a medium-size mixing bowl, stirring with a fork to moisten the crumbs. Spread the crumb mixture in the pan, and press them evenly into the bottom and up the sides of the pan.

3. To make the cake, in a food processor or using a hand mixer, process or beat the cream cheese and tofu together until smooth. Add the granulated sugar, cornstarch, coffee, brandy extract, and salt, blending until smooth. Pour the mixture evenly into the prepared pan. Cover with aluminum foil, making several holes in the foil for steam to escape. Place the pan on the rack, cover, and cook on High for 2½ to 3 hours, until firm.

4. Take the pan out of the cooker, remove the foil, and let it stand until cool. Once cool, cover and refrigerate for several hours or overnight. Chill completely before removing from the pan.

5. To serve, remove the sides of the pan, using a knife to loosen if necessary. Spread the top of the cheesecake with the chocolate curls.

6. To make the sauce, combine the confectioners' sugar, cocoa powder, coffee, and brandy in a small mixing bowl, stirring until smooth. Add more sugar if a sweeter sauce is desired. Spoon a pool of the sauce onto each dessert plate, then top with a slice of the cake.

Lemon-Lime Cheesecake with Gingersnap Crust

The light, crisp taste of citrus blended into the creamy filling makes this an ideal finale after a spicy meal. If you don't have a rack or trivet that fits inside the cooker, invert a small bowl to keep the cheesecake pan off the bottom of the cooker.

Slow Cooker Size:
6 quart

Cook Time:
2½ to 3 hours

Setting: High

Serves 8

Boiling water as needed

Crust

1½ cups gingersnap crumbs
¼ cup nonhydrogenated margarine, melted

Filling

8 ounces regular or tofu cream cheese
12 ounces silken tofu, drained
¾ cup sugar
Juice and chopped zest of 1 lemon
Juice and chopped zest of 1 lime
1 teaspoon pure vanilla extract
2 tablespoons cornstarch

Topping

½ cup sliced almonds, toasted (page 185)

1. Place a rack or trivet in a 6-quart slow cooker. Pour about $\frac{1}{2}$ inch of boiling water in the bottom of the cooker, cover, and turn the heat setting to High. Lightly oil a 7-inch springform pan.

2. To make the crust, combine the gingersnap crumbs and margarine in a medium-size mixing bowl, stirring with a fork to moisten. Pat the crumb mixture into the bottom and up the sides of the prepared pan.

3. To make the filling, blend the cream cheese, tofu, and sugar together until smooth and creamy using a blender, food processor, or hand mixer. Blend in the lemon and lime juices and zest, vanilla, and cornstarch until well combined. Pour the mixture evenly into the prepared crust. Cover with aluminum foil, making several holes in the foil for steam to escape. Place the pan on the rack, cover, and cook on High for $2\frac{1}{2}$ to 3 hours, until firm.

4. Take the pan out of the cooker, remove the foil, and let stand until cool. Once cool, cover and refrigerate for several hours or overnight. Chill completely before removing from the pan.

5. To serve, remove the sides of the pan, using a knife to loosen if necessary. Sprinkle the top of the cheesecake with the toasted almonds.

Worth-the-Wait Chocolate-Almond Cheesecake

The maddeningly delicious aroma of this scrumptious cheesecake will have you wanting to dig in long before it's ready to eat.

Slow Cooker Size:
6 quart

Cook Time:
2½ to 3 hours

Setting: High

Serves 8

Boiling water as needed

Crust

1½ cups crushed chocolate wafers
¼ cup nonhydrogenated margarine, melted

Cake

One 8-ounce package regular or tofu cream cheese
8 ounces silken tofu, drained
½ cup sugar
4 ounces semisweet chocolate, melted
1½ tablespoons cornstarch
1 teaspoon pure almond extract
Pinch of salt

Garnish

½ cup sliced almonds, toasted (page 185)
½ cup Easy Chocolate Curls (page 213)

1. Place a rack or trivet in a 6-quart slow cooker. Pour about $\frac{1}{2}$ inch of boiling water in the bottom of the cooker, cover, and turn the heat setting to High. Lightly oil a 7-inch springform pan.

2. To make the crust, combine the crumbs and margarine in a medium-size mixing bowl, stirring with a fork to moisten the crumbs. Spread the crumb mixture into the pan, and press it evenly into the bottom and up the side of the pan.

3. To make the cake, process or beat the cream cheese and tofu together until smooth using a food processor or a hand mixer. Add the sugar, chocolate, cornstarch, almond extract, and salt and blend until smooth. Pour the mixture evenly into the prepared pan. Cover with aluminum foil, making several holes in the foil for steam to escape. Place the pan on the rack, cover, and cook on High for $2\frac{1}{2}$ to 3 hours, until firm.

4. Take the pan out of the cooker, remove the foil, and let it stand until cool. Once cool, cover and refrigerate for several hours or overnight. Chill completely before removing from pan.

5. To serve, remove the sides of the pan, using a knife to loosen if necessary. Sprinkle the almonds on top of the cheesecake, mostly in the center, and sprinkle the chocolate curls around the perimeter of the top of the cake.

Peach–Blueberry Tumble

Similar to a fruit crumble, kind of like a fruit crisp, I call this a "tumble," because you basically tumble all the ingredients in a slow cooker, and in a couple of hours it's dessert.

Slow Cooker Size:
3½ to 4 quart

Cook Time: 2 hours

Setting: High

Serves 4

4 large ripe peaches, peeled (see Note on page 198), pitted, and sliced
1 cup fresh blueberries, picked over for stems
½ cup firmly packed light brown sugar or a natural sweetener
¾ cup rolled (old-fashioned) oats
⅓ cup nonhydrogenated margarine, softened
1 teaspoon ground cinnamon
¼ teaspoon salt

1. Place the peaches in a 3½- to 4-quart slow cooker. Add the blueberries and ¼ cup of the brown sugar and stir to combine.

2. In a medium-size mixing bowl, combine the remaining ¼ cup brown sugar, the oats, margarine, cinnamon, and salt. Mix well and sprinkle on top of the fruit.

3. Put the lid on the cooker slightly askew to let the steam escape. Cook on High for about 2 hours. If too much liquid remains, remove the lid and cook 30 minutes longer. Serve hot.

Know Your Grunts and Slumps

While you may know the difference between a pie and a tart, things may get a little hazy when it comes to other fruit desserts such as crumbles and grunts. Here's a rundown of the tasty fruity treats that can be made in a slow cooker:

Cobbler: A baked fruit dessert made in a deep baking dish and topped with a thick biscuit crust

Crisp: A baked fruit dessert with a crumbly pastry mixture topping made in a pie plate or other shallow baking dish

Crumble: A baked fruit dessert topped with a crumbly pastry mixture

Grunt: A stewed-fruit dessert with a biscuit topping, also known as a slump

Blueberry Cobbler

This cobbler is simple to make and cooks quickly for a slow-cooked recipe. I sometimes start it right before dinner and it's ready to serve fresh and warm not long after dinner is finished—just about the time we're ready for something sweet and delicious. It's an especially welcome way to make cobbler during the heat of summer when fresh blueberries are at their peak but you don't feel like working over a hot stove.

Slow Cooker Size:
3½ to 4 quart

Cook Time: 1½ hours

Setting: High

Serves 4

3 cups fresh blueberries, picked over for stems
½ cup sugar or a natural sweetener
1 tablespoon cornstarch
¼ cup boiling water
¾ cup unbleached all-purpose flour
1 teaspoon baking powder
Pinch of salt
Pinch of ground cinnamon
⅓ cup milk or soy milk
1 tablespoon corn oil or other mild-tasting oil

1. In a 3½- to 4-quart slow cooker, combine the blueberries, ¼ cup of the sugar, and the cornstarch, stirring to coat. Turn the heat setting to High and add the boiling water. Stir to combine.

2. In a small mixing bowl, combine the flour, the remaining ¼ cup sugar, the baking powder, salt, and cinnamon.

3. In another small mixing bowl, combine the milk and oil. Stir the wet ingredients into the dry ingredients until just combined. Spread the batter evenly over the blueberry mixture. Cover and cook on High for 1½ hours.

4. Remove the lid, turn the cooker off, and let the cobbler set for 20 minutes before serving.

Pieless Apples à la Mode

This slow-cooked apple-and-cinnamon mixture smells and tastes like apple pie but without the fuss (or the crust). I serve this comforting dessert warm with dairy-free vanilla ice cream.

Slow Cooker Size:
3½ to 4 quart

Cook Time:
3½ to 4 hours

Setting: Low

Serves 4 to 6

4 Granny Smith apples, peeled, cored, and thinly sliced
2 tablespoons unbleached all-purpose flour
½ cup firmly packed light brown sugar or a natural sweetener
½ teaspoon ground cinnamon
¼ cup golden raisins or sweetened dried cranberries (optional)
½ cup rolled (old-fashioned) oats
2 tablespoons nonhydrogenated margarine, softened
Vanilla ice cream (regular or dairy-free) for serving

1. In a large mixing bowl, combine the apples, flour, ¼ cup of the brown sugar, ¼ teaspoon of the cinnamon, and the raisins, if using. Stir to coat, then transfer the mixture to a lightly oiled 3½- to 4-quart slow cooker.

2. In a small mixing bowl, combine the oats, the remaining ¼ cup brown sugar, ¼ teaspoon cinnamon, and the margarine. Sprinkle the oat mixture over the apples. Cover and cook on Low for 3½ to 4 hours.

3. Serve warm, spooned into dessert dishes and topped with a scoop of ice cream.

Brandy-Laced Pear Brown Betty

Here's a new twist on the classic dessert apple brown Betty, but made with pears and spiked with brandy (or brandy extract, if you prefer). This tastes great served warm with a scoop of regular or dairy-free vanilla ice cream alongside. You may use your choice of Anjou, Bosc, or Bartlett pears.

Slow Cooker Size:
3½ to 4 quart

Cook Time: 3 hours

Setting: Low

Serves 6 to 8

4 cups cubed white bread
¾ cup firmly packed light brown sugar or a natural sweetener
¼ cup pure maple syrup
2 tablespoons corn oil or other mild-tasting oil
½ teaspoon ground cinnamon
¼ teaspoon ground allspice
¼ teaspoon ground ginger
¼ teaspoon ground nutmeg
⅛ teaspoon salt
4 medium-size ripe pears, peeled, cored, and chopped
2 tablespoons brandy or 1 tablespoon brandy extract
1 tablespoon fresh lemon juice

1. In a large mixing bowl, combine the bread cubes, brown sugar, maple syrup, oil, spices, and salt.

2. In a medium-size mixing bowl, combine the pears, brandy, and lemon juice.

3. Lightly oil a 3½- to 4-quart slow cooker and arrange the bread mixture and then the pear mixture in two alternating layers. Cover and cook on Low for 3 hours, until firm. Serve hot.

Ginger–Pineapple Bread Pudding

This homey bread pudding spiced with ginger and cinnamon is studded with pineapple for a taste of the tropics. A sprinkling of toasted coconut complements the flavors nicely.

Slow Cooker Size:
3½ to 4 quart

Cook Time: 3 hours

Setting: Low

Serves 6 to 8

4 cups cubed white bread

3 cups peeled, cored, and chopped fresh pineapple or two 16-ounce cans crushed pineapple, well drained

¾ cup firmly packed light brown sugar or a natural sweetener

1 teaspoon ground cinnamon

½ teaspoon ground ginger

1 teaspoon vanilla extract

⅛ teaspoon salt

¾ cup unsweetened coconut milk

Toasted unsweetened coconut (page 215; optional)

1. Press half of the bread cubes into the bottom of a lightly oiled 3½- to 4-quart slow cooker.

2. In a large mixing bowl, combine the pineapple, brown sugar, cinnamon, ginger, vanilla, and salt. Mix well, then stir in the coconut milk.

3. Pour half the pineapple mixture over the bread in the slow cooker, pressing the bread pieces down to moisten them. Repeat with remaining bread and pineapple mixture. Cover and cook on Low for 3 hours, until firm.

4. Turn off the slow cooker and let the pudding rest, covered, for 20 minutes before serving. Garnish with coconut, if desired.

Bourbon-Spiked Pumpkin Bread Pudding

Pumpkin bread pudding is a cold weather favorite in our house. It's great for a crowd at holiday gatherings, when you want the seasonal taste of pumpkin without the fuss of a pie.

Slow Cooker Size:
3½ to 4 quart

Cook Time: 3 hours

Setting: Low

Serves 6 to 8

4 cups cubed white bread

3 cups milk or vanilla soy milk

One 16-ounce can solid-pack pumpkin

¾ cup firmly packed light brown sugar or a natural sweetener

¼ cup bourbon

1 teaspoon pure vanilla extract

1½ teaspoons ground cinnamon

½ teaspoon ground ginger

¼ teaspoon ground allspice

¼ teaspoon ground nutmeg

¼ teaspoon salt

1. Press half the bread cubes into the bottom of a lightly oiled 3½- to 4-quart slow cooker.

2. In a medium-size saucepan, heat the milk until hot, but do not let it come to a boil. Remove the pan from the heat and set aside.

3. In a large mixing bowl, combine the pumpkin, brown sugar, bourbon, vanilla, spices, and salt. Blend well, then slowly add the hot milk, stirring constantly. Carefully pour half the pumpkin mixture over the bread and push the bread pieces down beneath the mixture to moisten them. Repeat with remaining bread and pumpkin mixture. Cover and cook on Low for 3 hours, until firm.

4. Turn off the slow cooker and let the pudding sit, covered, for 20 minutes before serving.

Fudgy Chocolate Pudding Cake

Served warm, this dessert is more like pudding, but as it cools, it becomes more cake-like. Whether you call it a cake or a pudding, it's easy to make and so chocolatey that it gives you that "warm fudgy" feeling. Serve with regular or dairy-free vanilla ice cream.

Slow Cooker Size:
6 quart

Cook Time: 3 hours

Setting: High

Serves 4 to 6

2 cups boiling water
1 cup sugar or a natural sweetener
2 tablespoons corn oil or other mild-tasting oil
1½ cups milk or chocolate or vanilla soy milk
½ teaspoon vanilla extract or liqueur of choice
1 cup unbleached all-purpose flour
½ cup unsweetened cocoa powder
2 teaspoons baking powder
¼ teaspoon salt
Toasted slivered almonds (page 185)

1. Place a rack or trivet in a 6-quart slow cooker. Pour in the boiling water, cover, and turn the heat setting to High. Lightly oil a baking dish that will fit inside the cooker.

2. In a large mixing bowl, beat the sugar and oil together until well blended. Stir in the milk and vanilla.

3. In a small mixing bowl, combine the flour, cocoa, baking powder, and salt. Fold the dry ingredients into the wet ingredients until just blended. Pour the batter into the prepared dish and cover tightly with aluminum foil, making several holes in the foil for steam to escape. Set it on the rack, cover, and cook on High for 3 hours, until a toothpick inserted in the center comes out clean.

4. Let stand at least 10 minutes before serving. Garnish with almonds and serve warm or at room temperature.

Chocolate Fantasy Fondue

Like slow cookers, fondues are back in vogue, and with this chocolate lover's fantasy you can make your fondue right in your slow cooker. What could be better than a pot of warm, rich chocolate laced with your favorite liqueur just waiting for you to dip in chunks of cake, fruit, and any other yummy treats you desire?

Slow Cooker Size:
1 to 1½ quarts

Cook Time: 1 hour

Setting: High

Serves 6

12 ounces semisweet chocolate

¾ cup milk or vanilla soy milk

2 tablespoons liqueur of choice (optional; Amaretto or Frangelico are good choices)

Assorted fresh fruit for dipping, cut into bite-size pieces as necessary (strawberries, bananas, cherries, pineapple, etc.)

Firm cake or cookies, cut into bite-size pieces (pretzels are also fun)

1. Break the chocolate into pieces and place in a 1- to 1½-quart slow cooker. Add the milk and liqueur, if using. Turn the cooker on High and cook, uncovered, for about an hour. Stir occasionally until smooth, adding a little more milk if the consistency is too thick.

2. Bring the "fondue pot" (a.k.a. slow cooker) to the table along with fondue forks or wooden skewers. Arrange the fruit and cake on platters and set them on the table so that guests may help themselves to the selection, which they can skewer and dip into the chocolate.

Slow-Baked Apples

This healthful and easy dessert fills the house with a wonderful "apple pie" aroma as it cooks. I also like to serve baked apples as a side dish with certain meals, such as Not Your Mama's Pot Roast (page 130).

Slow Cooker Size:
3½ to 6 quart
(depending on the
number of apples)

Cook Time: 3 to 4 hours

Setting: Low

Serves 4 to 6

4 to 6 firm cooking apples, such as Granny Smith or Rome Beauty, cored
Juice of 1 lemon
¼ cup firmly packed light brown sugar or a natural sweetener
1 teaspoon ground cinnamon
2 tablespoons nonhydrogenated margarine
½ cup apple juice

1. Peel the apples about one-third of the way down from the top. Rub the exposed part of the apples with the lemon juice so they don't discolor.

2. Place the apples upright in a 3½- to 6-quart slow cooker. Sprinkle with the brown sugar and cinnamon and dot with the margarine. Pour in the apple juice. Cover and cook on Low for 3 to 4 hours, until the apples are tender. These apples are delicious served hot, chilled, or at room temperature.

Apples Stuffed with Cranberries and Almond Butter

These baked apples have a surprise inside—a yummy concoction of dried cranberries, almonds, and spices.

Slow Cooker Size:
5½ to 6 quart

Cook Time: 3 to 4 hours

Setting: Low

Serves 6

6 cooking apples, such as Granny Smith or Rome Beauty, cored
Juice of 1 lemon
3 tablespoons unbleached all-purpose flour
3 tablespoons sugar or a natural sweetener
½ teaspoon ground cinnamon
⅛ teaspoon salt
3 tablespoons almond butter
1 tablespoon nonhydrogenated margarine
½ cup sweetened dried cranberries
¼ cup chopped almonds
⅔ cup cranberry juice cocktail
⅔ cup water

1. Peel the apples about one-third of the way down from the top. Rub the exposed part of the apples with the lemon juice so they don't discolor.

2. In a small mixing bowl, combine the flour, sugar, cinnamon, salt, almond butter, and margarine until crumbly. Add the cranberries and chopped almonds and mix well. Stuff the mixture into the center of each apple and place them upright in a 5½- to 6-quart slow cooker. Sprinkle any remaining stuffing mixture on top of the apples.

3. Combine the cranberry juice and water and pour around the apples. Cover and cook on Low for 3 to 4 hours, until the apples are tender. Serve warm.

Slow Cooker Poached Pears

For a more sophisticated version, red or white wine may be substituted for the white grape or cranberry juice. You can use any pear you like, such as Bartlett or Anjou, but I find that Boscs hold up best when prepared whole.

Slow Cooker Size:
4 quart

Cook Time: 3 to 4 hours

Setting: Low

Serves 4

⅓ cup firmly packed light brown sugar or a natural sweetener
1 teaspoon ground cinnamon
2 cups white grape juice or cranberry juice cocktail
4 just-ripe pears
Juice of 1 lemon

1. Combine the brown sugar, cinnamon, and juice in a 4-quart slow cooker, stirring to dissolve the sugar.

2. Remove the peel from the top half of the pears, leaving the stem end intact. Rub with the lemon juice to prevent discoloration. Cut a slice off the bottom of the pears so they stand evenly. Arrange the pears upright in the slow cooker. Cover and cook on Low for 3 to 4 hours, until the pears are just tender. Do not overcook.

3. With a slotted spoon, remove the pears to a plate to cool. Turn the heat setting on the cooker to High and cook, uncovered, to reduce the poaching liquid by half. Pour the reduced liquid into a heatproof bowl and let it cool.

4. To serve, arrange a whole poached pear on a small plate and drizzle it with the reduced poaching liquid. Serve at room temperature for the best flavor.

Breakfast and Bread

. . .

To many people, breakfast means grabbing a "quick" this or an "instant" that—certainly not something that takes hours to cook in a slow cooker. But when you put it on the night before, a slow-cooked breakfast can be even more convenient than a grab-and-go alternative.

Many of these breakfast recipes made with nutritious whole grains can cook during the overnight hours so they're ready by morning. Others take only a few hours to cook so, unless you have an early riser in your house who can turn on the cooker before everyone else gets up, the simplest solution is to plug your cooker into an automatic timer. Available at hardware stores, a kitchen appliance timer allows you to set your slow cooker to begin cooking up to two hours after you go to bed. (Uncooked food should not be left at room temperature for longer than two hours.)

The breads in this chapter could be called "slow quick breads" for they are literally quick breads that are made in a slow cooker. Boston brown bread, traditionally steam-baked in a pot, is a natural for the slow cooker, but you will find that the cornbread, pumpkin bread, and even a delightful cranberry-walnut bread also turn out just fine using this method.

Maple-Almond Granola with Cranberries and Dates

Homemade granola is more economical than commercial brands and also tastes better because you make it fresh yourself and you can customize the ingredients. For example, substitute dried blueberries for the cranberries, use raisins instead of dates, or omit the coconut in favor of something you like better. Granola is also easy to make in a slow cooker because you don't have to worry about it burning in the oven.

Slow Cooker Size:
4 quart

Cook Time: 3½ hours

Setting: 1½ hours on High; 2 hours on Low

Makes about 8 cups

5 cups rolled (old-fashioned) oats
1 cup sliced almonds
¾ cup sweetened dried cranberries
¾ cup unsweetened shredded coconut
½ cup chopped dates
½ cup sesame seeds
⅔ cup pure maple syrup
¼ cup corn oil or other mild-tasting oil
¼ teaspoon ground cinnamon
Pinch of salt

1. Combine all the ingredients in a lightly oiled 4-quart slow cooker and stir to combine. Cook on High for 1½ hours, uncovered, stirring occasionally.

2. Reduce the heat to Low and cook, uncovered, for 2 hours, stirring occasionally, until the mixture is crisp and dry.

3. Spread the granola on a baking sheet to cool completely. Store in airtight jars. It will taste best if used within 2 weeks.

Old-Fashioned Apple-Raisin Oatmeal

Slow cooking results in a super-creamy oatmeal. To appease those who prefer some texture in their oatmeal, granola is sprinkled on at serving time, which also lends sweetness to the hot cereal. Enlist a kitchen timer to start your cooker an hour or so after you go to bed so the oatmeal will be ready when you arise.

Slow Cooker Size:
3½ to 4 quart

Cook Time: 6 hours

Setting: Low

Serves 6

1½ cups rolled (old-fashioned) oats
4 cups cold water
1 teaspoon salt
1 teaspoon ground cinnamon
1 medium-size cooking apple, such as Granny Smith or Rome Beauty, cored, peeled, and shredded
3 tablespoons raisins
½ cup granola, or to taste

1. Combine all the ingredients except the granola in a lightly oiled 3½- to 4-quart slow cooker. Cover and cook on Low for 6 hours.

2. To serve, spoon the oatmeal into bowls, sprinkle with the granola, and serve hot.

Tried-and-True Favorite Toppings for Hot Cereals

Maple syrup

Granola

Toasted chopped nuts

Raisins

Sunflower seeds

Ground flax seeds

Toasted sesame seeds

Dried cranberries

Chopped fresh apple, pear, and/or peach

Fresh berries

Sliced bananas

Chopped dried plums

Cinnamon and sugar

Fruit jam or preserves

Dark unsulfured molasses

Barley and Kamut Breakfast Pilaf

Put this delicious stick-to-your-ribs breakfast pilaf together the night before and let it cook all night, awakening to its warming fragrance on a cold winter morning. Soak the kamut in water for 6 to 8 hours before cooking to soften slightly.

Slow Cooker Size:
3½ to 4 quart

Cook Time: 6 to 8 hours

Setting: Low

Serves 4

⅓ cup kamut, soaked in water to cover 6 to 8 hours
⅓ cup pearl barley
¼ cup rolled (old-fashioned) oats
2 tablespoons cornmeal
½ cup chopped mixed dried fruit
½ teaspoon ground cinnamon
½ teaspoon salt
4 cups water
1 teaspoon vanilla extract
Pure maple syrup for serving

1. In a 3½- to 4-quart slow cooker, combine the kamut, barley, oats, and cornmeal. Stir in the dried fruit, cinnamon, and salt, then stir in the water and vanilla. Cover and cook 6 to 8 hours on Low.

2. Stir, then spoon into bowls and drizzle with maple syrup.

Cream of Wheat Berries with Cranberries and Cardamom

Combine these great grains the night before so breakfast is ready when you are the next morning. This fragrant, hot cereal is good served with a little maple syrup or brown sugar and a splash of vanilla soy milk. Cinnamon or allspice may be used instead of cardamom, if you prefer.

Slow Cooker Size:
3½ to 4 quart

Cook Time: 6 to 8 hours

Setting: Low

Serves 4

½ cup wheat berries
¼ cup cracked wheat
½ cup rolled (old-fashioned) oats
4 cups water
½ teaspoon salt
¼ teaspoon ground cardamom
½ cup sweetened dried cranberries

1. In a 3½- to 4-quart slow cooker, combine the wheat berries, cracked wheat, oats, and water. Stir in the salt and cardamom. Cover and cook on Low for 6 to 8 hours.

2. Stir in the cranberries just before serving.

Good Morning Millet Mélange

The subtle sweet taste of millet combines well with dried and fresh fruit for an enticing way to start the day.

Slow Cooker Size:
4 quart

Cook Time: 6 hours

Setting: Low

Serves 4

1 cup millet
1 cup chopped dried fruit of your choice
1 ripe pear, peeled, cored, and chopped
1 teaspoon peeled and grated fresh ginger
3 cups apple juice
1 cup water
½ teaspoon salt

1. Place the millet in a small dry skillet and cook over medium heat, stirring constantly, until toasted, about 5 minutes. Be careful not to burn it.

2. Transfer the millet to a 4-quart slow cooker and add the remaining ingredients. Cover and cook on Low for 6 hours.

Congee Anytime

A congee is a rice porridge served as a breakfast food in China, but it can also be enjoyed at other times of the day. Serve it accompanied by small bowls of condiments to be added according to personal taste. Almost any rice can be used to make congee; however, Arborio will produce the creamiest texture.

Slow Cooker Size:
3½ to 4 quart

Cook Time: 6 to 8 hours

Setting: Low

Serves 6

1 cup Arborio or other rice
1 small yellow onion, minced
1 cup finely shredded Napa cabbage
1 tablespoon peeled and minced fresh ginger
1 garlic clove, minced
6 cups vegetable stock (see A Note About Stock, page 32)
1 tablespoon tamari or other soy sauce, plus more to serve
Chopped scallions for garnish
Chopped dry-roasted peanuts for garnish

1. In a 3½- to 4-quart slow cooker, combine the rice, onion, cabbage, ginger, and garlic. Stir in the stock and tamari. Cover and cook on Low for 6 to 8 hours, until the texture is thick and creamy.

2. To serve, ladle the congee into soup bowls and garnish with scallions and peanuts. Put extra tamari on the table for people to add according to taste.

Cornmeal Porridge with Almonds and Dates

Cornmeal has many different food personalities. It can be dressed up for dinner by being made into polenta or baked as cornbread. It can also be served for breakfast when it is called porridge, which certainly has a nicer ring to it than "mush," a decidedly unflattering title. In this recipe, basic cornmeal porridge is elevated with the embellishments of toasted almonds, chopped dates, and a drizzle of maple syrup.

Slow Cooker Size:
3½ to 4 quart

Cook Time: 6 hours

Setting: Low

Serves 4

1½ cups medium- or coarse-ground cornmeal
5 cups water
¾ teaspoon salt
½ cup chopped dates
½ cup slivered almonds, toasted (page 185)
Pure maple syrup for serving

1. Combine the cornmeal, water, salt, and dates in a 3½- to 4-quart slow cooker. Cover and cook on Low for 6 hours.

2. When the porridge is ready to serve, stir in the almonds. Spoon into bowls and drizzle with maple syrup as desired.

Breakfast Bread Pudding

Bits of apple and soy sausage dot this casserole, which can be assembled in advance and put in the cooker just before going to bed. Because it cooks in about six hours, however, it's best made in a slow cooker that has an automatic Keep Warm setting if you like to sleep in. It can also be served for brunch, lunch, or as a light supper.

Slow Cooker Size:
4 quart

Cook Time: 6 hours

Setting: Low

Serves 4 to 6

4½ cups cubed French or Italian bread

3 large cooking apples, such as Granny Smith or Rome Beauty, cored, peeled, and chopped

1 teaspoon ground cinnamon

½ teaspoon ground allspice

¼ cup firmly packed light brown sugar

¼ teaspoon salt

2 cups milk or soy milk

¼ cup pure maple syrup

12 ounces cooked soy sausage, crumbled

1. Press half the bread cubes into the bottom of a lightly oiled 4-quart slow cooker.

2. In a large mixing bowl, combine the apples, cinnamon, allspice, brown sugar, and salt. Pour on the milk and maple syrup, stirring to blend.

3. Carefully pour half the apple mixture over the bread and push the bread pieces down beneath the mixture to moisten them. Top with half the sausage, the remaining bread, the remaining sausage, followed by the remaining apple mixture. Press down to be sure the bread is moistened. Cover and cook on Low for 6 hours.

Slow Fruit Compote

This nutritious and flavorful compote made with fresh and dried fruit is a great way to start your day.

Slow Cooker Size:
4 quart

Cook Time: 4 hours

Setting: Low

Serves 6

1 cinnamon stick, broken into pieces
½ teaspoon whole cloves
½ teaspoon allspice berries
2 Granny Smith apples, cored, peeled, and cut into bite-size pieces
2 ripe pears, peeled, cored, and cut into bite-size pieces
8 ounces mixed dried fruit, cut into bite-size pieces
4 ounces pitted dried plums (prunes), cut in half
¼ cup sugar or natural sweetener
Grated zest and juice of 1 orange
2 cups water

1. Place the cinnamon, cloves, and allspice in the center of a 6-inch square piece of cheesecloth. Gather the ends of the cloth together and tie with string to enclose the spices.

2. Combine all the ingredients, including the spice bag, in a 4-quart slow cooker. Cover and cook on Low until the fruit is soft and the liquid is syrupy, about 4 hours.

3. Set aside to cool, then transfer to a bowl, cover, and refrigerate for several hours or until ready to use. Remove and discard the spice bag. The compote tastes best when served at room temperature and if used within a week.

Boston Brown Bread

This soft, luscious bread made with nutrient-rich walnuts, molasses, and raisins is a great way to start your day. Slather it with almond butter and sprinkle with ground flax seeds for a dynamo of nutrition.

Slow Cooker Size:
6 quart

Cook Time:
3½ to 4 hours

Setting: High

Makes 1 loaf

2 cups boiling water
1¼ cups milk or soy milk
1½ tablespoons cider vinegar
2 cups unbleached all-purpose flour
1 cup medium- or coarse-ground cornmeal
1 teaspoon salt
1 teaspoon baking soda
¾ cup dark unsulfured molasses
½ cup coarsely chopped walnuts
½ cup raisins

1. Place a trivet or rack inside a 6-quart slow cooker and add the boiling water. Turn the cooker on High. Lightly oil a baking pan that will fit inside your cooker and set aside.

2. In a small mixing bowl or measuring cup, combine the milk and vinegar and set aside.

3. In a large mixing bowl, combine the flour, cornmeal, salt, and baking soda. Mix well. Add the molasses and soured milk mixture and stir until the batter is just mixed. Stir in the walnuts and raisins with a few quick strokes.

4. Transfer the batter to the prepared pan and place on the trivet in the slow cooker. Cover and cook on High until firm and a toothpick inserted in the center comes out dry, 3½ to 4 hours. Let cool in the pan for 10 minutes before slicing. This bread tastes best served warm, soon after it is made.

Pumpkin-Pecan Bread

Keep a loaf of this bread on hand during the holidays for drop-in guests or to bring along when you visit others—it makes a lovely holiday gift when wrapped in plastic wrap and tied with ribbon. Serve it warm or cool, unadorned or spread with a nut butter or tofu cream cheese.

Slow Cooker Size:
5½ to 6 quart

Cook Time: 3 hours

Setting: High

Makes 1 loaf

2 cups boiling water
¼ cup corn oil or other mild-tasting oil
½ cup firmly packed light brown sugar
1 cup canned pumpkin purée
2 large eggs or egg replacement mixture for 2 eggs
1¾ cups unbleached all-purpose flour
2 teaspoons baking powder
½ teaspoon salt
½ cup chopped pecans

1. Place a trivet or rack inside the slow cooker and add the boiling water. Turn the cooker on High. Lightly oil a small loaf pan or other baking pan that will fit inside a 5½- to 6-quart slow cooker and set aside.

2. In a medium-size mixing bowl, combine the oil, brown sugar, pumpkin, and eggs or egg replacement mixture and mix well.

3. In a large mixing bowl, sift together the flour, baking powder, and salt. Stir in the wet ingredients, blending well. Stir in the nuts.

4. Transfer the batter to the prepared pan and cover tightly with aluminum foil. Poke a few holes in the foil to allow the steam to escape, then place the pan on the trivet, cover, and cook on High until the bread is firm and a toothpick inserted in the center comes out clean, about 3 hours.

Maple-Sweetened Cornbread

Cornbread is delicious at any time of day. It can be served as an accompaniment to chili or other stew for lunch or dinner or served at breakfast with a hot cup of tea or coffee. Try it spread with apple butter for a real treat.

Slow Cooker Size:
5½ to 6 quart

Cook Time: 3 to 4 hours

Setting: High

Makes 1 loaf

2 cups boiling water
1¼ cups medium- or coarse-ground cornmeal
1 cup unbleached all-purpose flour
2½ teaspoons baking powder
1 teaspoon salt
1 cup milk or soy milk
¼ cup pure maple syrup
¼ cup corn oil

1. Place a trivet or rack inside a 5½- to 6-quart slow cooker and add the boiling water. Turn the cooker on High. Lightly oil a baking pan that will fit inside your cooker.

2. In a large mixing bowl, combine the cornmeal, flour, baking powder, and salt.

3. In a small mixing bowl or measuring cup, combine the milk, maple syrup, and oil. Add the wet ingredients to the dry ingredients and mix well with a few quick strokes.

4. Transfer the batter to the prepared pan and place on the trivet in the slow cooker. Cover and cook on High until firm and a toothpick inserted in the center comes out dry, 3 to 4 hours. Serve hot or warm.

Cranberry-Walnut Breakfast Bread

Because of the variety of healthful ingredients, this bread makes an ideal breakfast loaf. For added nutrition, spread slices with a nut butter and sprinkle with ground flax seeds.

Slow Cooker Size:
5½ to 6 quart

Cook Time: 3 to 4 hours

Setting: High

Makes 1 loaf

2 cups boiling water
⅓ cup corn oil or other mild-tasting oil
½ cup firmly packed light brown sugar
1 large ripe banana, mashed
2 large eggs or egg replacement mixture for 2 eggs
1¾ cups unbleached all-purpose flour
2 teaspoons baking powder
½ teaspoon salt
½ cup chopped walnuts
½ cup sweetened dried cranberries

1. Place a trivet or rack inside a 5½- to 6-quart slow cooker and add the boiling water. Turn the cooker on High. Lightly oil a small loaf pan or other baking pan that will fit inside the cooker and set aside.

2. In a large mixing bowl, combine the oil, brown sugar, banana, and eggs or egg replacement mixture and mix well.

3. In a medium-size mixing bowl, sift together the flour, baking powder, and salt. Add the dry ingredients to the wet ingredients and mix well. Stir in the nuts and cranberries.

4. Pour the batter into the prepared pan and cover tightly with aluminum foil. Poke a few holes in the foil to allow the steam to escape, then place the pan on the trivet, cover, and cook on High until firm and a toothpick inserted in the center comes out dry, 3 to 4 hours. Let cool for 10 to 15 minutes before removing from the pan.

Hot Drinks from the Electric Punch Bowl

. . .

*Winter gatherings of all kinds can be the perfect oc-*casions to serve warm beverages. Whether you whip up a steaming pot of spiced cider at a Halloween party, a festive wassail punch for a cup of holiday cheer, or some soothing ginger-spiked peach tea "just because," hot beverages can add a special touch to any gathering. Slow cookers are ideal for this purpose because they will keep your drink warm throughout the evening and can be placed right on a buffet table, freeing you from monitoring a bubbling pot on the stove.

Mulled wine is great anytime, especially a cozy evening for two in front of the fireplace. Best of all, these drinks can be served piping hot directly from the slow cooker into waiting mugs or heat-proof punch cups. Since a slow cooker maintains a good serving temperature for several hours, it's like having an electric punch bowl. It also can be convenient when you go out for a few hours—for a family sledding expedition, for example—and want to come home to a nice hot drink without the wait. Thanks to the electric punch bowl, it's also great to not have to worry about reheating or refilling hot beverages at parties.

Spiced Hot Mocha

Inspired by an Italian dessert where hot espresso is poured over a scoop of gelato, this decadent concoction is like having coffee and dessert rolled into one. Add the brandy or not at your own discretion—it's delicious either way.

Slow Cooker Size:
3½ to 4 quart

Cook Time: 1 to 2 hours

Setting: Low

Makes about 6½ cups

1 pint chocolate regular or dairy-free ice cream (Tofutti is a good choice)
4 cups hot coffee
½ cup brandy, or to taste (optional)
Ground cinnamon for garnish

1. Place the ice cream in a 3½- to 4-quart slow cooker. Pour the hot coffee over the ice cream, stirring to melt. Cover and cook on Low for 1 to 2 hours. Stir in the brandy, if using.

2. To serve, ladle into mugs and garnish with a sprinkle of cinnamon.

Note: This recipe is easily doubled for a crowd.

Ginger-Peach Spiked Tea

This fragrant and flavorful hot drink will keep at a good serving temperature for several hours. To serve it "unspiked," simply omit the ginger brandy. If you can't find peach tea, substitute another complementary tea, such as an herbal lemon tea or even regular orange pekoe tea. You could also use ginger tea to intensify the ginger flavor.

Slow Cooker Size:
3½ to 4 quart

Cook Time: 1 to 2 hours

Setting: Low

**Makes about
2 quarts**

¼ cup loose peach tea leaves
1 quart boiling water
8 slices fresh ginger
½ cup firmly packed light brown sugar
1 quart peach juice
¼ cup fresh lemon juice
½ cup ginger brandy
Thinly sliced lemon for garnish (optional)

1. Combine the tea and boiling water in a teapot or other heatproof container until steeped, about 10 minutes.

2. Strain the tea into the slow cooker and add the fresh ginger, brown sugar, peach juice, and lemon juice. Cover and cook on Low until hot, 1 to 2 hours.

3. When ready to serve, scoop the ginger slices out of the liquid and add the ginger brandy. Turn the heat down to the Keep Warm setting if your slow cooker has that function; otherwise, keep it on Low to serve. Float lemon slices on the top, if desired.

Hot Cranberry Punch

This festive-looking punch is a hit at any gathering. For a spiked version, add a generous splash of vodka to the cooker when ready to serve.

Slow Cooker Size:
3½ to 4 quart

Cook Time: 1 to 2 hours

Setting: Low

**Makes about
2 quarts**

2 cinnamon sticks, broken into pieces
1 teaspoon whole cloves
1 teaspoon allspice berries
4 cups cranberry juice cocktail
2 cups apple juice
½ cup firmly packed light brown sugar
2 tablespoons fresh lemon juice
1 medium-size orange, sliced

1. Place the cinnamon, cloves, and allspice in the center of a 6-inch square piece of cheesecloth. Gather the ends of the cloth together and tie with a string to enclose the spices.

2. Combine the cranberry juice, apple juice, and brown sugar in a 3½- to 4-quart slow cooker and stir to dissolve the sugar. Stir in the lemon juice and add the spice bag. Cover and cook on Low for 1 to 2 hours.

3. Just before serving, remove and discard the spice bag and float the orange slices on the top. Serve hot.

Hot Spiced Cider

The first cold nip of autumn is occasion enough to put on a pot of this warming cider.

Slow Cooker Size:
3½ to 4 quart

Cook Time: 2 hours

Setting: Low

Makes 2 quarts

2 cinnamon sticks
1 teaspoon whole cloves
1 teaspoon allspice berries
2 quarts apple cider
½ cup firmly packed light brown sugar
1 medium-size orange, sliced

1. Place the cinnamon, cloves, and allspice in the center of a 6-inch square piece of cheesecloth and tie it up with string to enclose the spices.

2. Combine the cider and brown sugar in a 3½- to 4-quart slow cooker and stir to dissolve the sugar. Add the spice bag. Cover and cook on Low for 2 hours.

3. Before serving, remove the spice bag and float the orange slices in the hot cider. Serve hot.

Mulled Wine

Anyone who has tried to keep a pot of mulled wine going on the kitchen stove during a holiday party will appreciate the convenience of this slow cooker version. Put it together, turn it on, and then forget it. Guests can help themselves and the wine stays at the perfect serving temperature for hours.

Slow Cooker Size:
3½ to 4 quart

Cook Time: 2 to 3 hours

Setting: Low

Makes about 2 quarts

12 cloves
1 large orange
Two 4-inch cinnamon sticks
¾ cup firmly packed light brown sugar
Two 750-ml bottles dry red wine

1. Press the cloves into the orange and place it in a 3½- to 4-quart slow cooker.

2. Add the cinnamon, sugar, and wine, stirring to dissolve the sugar. Cover and cook on Low for 2 to 3 hours.

3. Just before serving, remove the cinnamon sticks. Serve hot.

Slow Cooker Swedish Glogg

Many versions of this traditional Swedish holiday drink exist—one more potent than the next. Some use aquavit, a Scandinavian liquor flavored with caraway seeds, while other versions call for vodka, combined variously with port, dry red wine, and even brandy. It's okay to use less expensive varieties of spirits for this potion since the good stuff would be masked by the aromatic spices.

Slow Cooker Size:
3½ to 4 quart

Cooking Time: 2 hours

Setting: Low

**Makes about
2 quarts**

12 cloves
3 cardamom pods, crushed
2 cinnamon sticks
3 slices fresh ginger
1 cup sugar
One 750-ml bottle dry red wine
Grated zest of 1 medium-size orange
One 750-ml bottle port
2 cups vodka or brandy
⅓ cup golden raisins
⅓ cup slivered almonds

1. Place the cloves, cardamom, cinnamon, and ginger in the center of a 6-inch square piece of cheesecloth and tie it up with string to enclose the spices.

2. Combine the sugar and wine in a 3½- to 4-quart slow cooker and stir to dissolve the sugar. Add the spice bag, orange zest, and port. Cover and cook on Low for 2 hours.

3. Shortly before serving, stir in the vodka, raisins, and almonds. Serve hot, ladling a few raisins and almonds into each serving.

Lemon-Ginger Sake-Toddy

If you're looking for something notably different from the usual punches, this may fit the bill. Sake, Japanese rice wine, lends a sophisticated flavor and is complemented by the added zip of ginger and touch of lemon. To support the Asian theme, serve this bracing toddy in Japanese teacups.

Slow Cooker Size:
3½ to 4 quart

Cook Time: 2 hours

Setting: Low

Makes 2 quarts

2 tablespoons chopped crystallized ginger
2 tablespoons firmly packed light brown sugar
Juice and grated zest of 1 lemon
1 quart sake
1 quart ginger ale

In a 3½- to 4-quart slow cooker, combine the ginger, brown sugar, lemon juice, and lemon zest. Add the sake and ginger ale and stir until the sugar dissolves. Cover and cook on Low for 2 hours. Serve hot.

Holiday Wassail

Named after the old Norse toast meaning "be in good health," wassail is usually made with ale and a generous splash of sherry, but I prefer to lace it with dark rum. Orange slices replace the customary garnish of small roasted apples and, of course, the slow cooker becomes the new "wassail bowl."

Slow Cooker Size:
3½ to 4 quart

Cook Time: 2 hours

Setting: Low

Makes about
2 quarts

4 cinnamon sticks
1 teaspoon whole cloves
1 cup water
¾ cup firmly packed light brown sugar
One 6-ounce can frozen lemonade concentrate, thawed
3 cups apple juice or cider
Two 12-ounce bottles ale
¾ cup dark rum
1 medium-size orange, sliced

1. Place the cinnamon and cloves in the center of a 6-inch square piece of cheesecloth and tie it up with string to enclose the spices.

2. Combine the water and brown sugar in a 3½- to 4-quart slow cooker and stir to dissolve the sugar. Stir in the lemonade concentrate. Stir in the apple juice and ale and add the spice bag. Cover and cook on Low for 2 hours.

3. Just before serving, remove and discard the spice bag and stir in the rum. Float the orange slices in the wassail and serve hot.

Origin of "the Toast"

The term *toast* is believed to have originated in seventeenth-century England where a small piece of toasted bread was placed in the wine goblet, supposedly to improve the flavor of the wine. The goblet would be passed among the guests until it reached the person being honored, who would take the final sip and eat the wine-soaked bread. Toasted bread was also placed in the traditional wassail bowl, along with roasted apples.

Alcohol-Free Wassail Punch

This nontraditional wassail is made with fruit juice and seasoned with spices for a re-freshing alcohol-free punch that truly embraces the meaning of *wassail*—"be in good health."

Slow Cooker Size:
3½ to 4 quart

Cook Time: 2 hours

Setting: Low

**Makes about
2 quarts**

1 teaspoon whole cloves
1 teaspoon allspice berries
2 cinnamon sticks, broken into 2-inch pieces
1½ quarts apple cider or juice
2 cups cranberry juice cocktail
One 6-ounce can frozen orange juice concentrate, thawed
1 orange, sliced

1. Place the cloves, allspice, and cinnamon in the center of a 6-inch square piece of cheesecloth and tie it up with string to enclose the spices.

2. In a 3½ - to 4-quart slow cooker, combine the cider, cranberry juice, and orange juice concentrate. Add the spice bag to the cider mixture. Cover and cook on Low until hot, about 2 hours.

3. Remove and discard the spice bag. Float the orange slices in the hot wassail. Serve hot.

Index